I Count My Blessings

Each Day is a Gift, a Blessing, a Connection

Eunice Nordby Simonson

Kirk House Publishers
Minneapolis, Minnesota

I Count My Blessings
Each Day is a Gift, a Blessing, a Connection

Eunice Nordby Simonson

ISBN - 10: 1-933794-34-8
ISBN - 13: 978-1-933794-34-1

LCCN: 2010941466

Kirk House Publishers, PO Box 390759. Minneapolis, MM 55439
www.kirkhouse.com
Manufactured in the United States of America.

Contents

Chapter 1 Early Years in North Dakota
Early Childhood 11
The First Parsonage 16
Primrose # 2 19
Let the Beauty 29
The Death of a Friend 30
In Winter I Get Up By Night 32
Bang, Perry, and Sherbrook 33
The First Call 35

Chapter 2 Years of Education
Oak Grove 37
Concordia Connection 41
Fairview 44

Chapter 3 Love and Marriage
Wedding, June 14, 1952 47
The Honeymoon 49
Hillside Attic 51
Luther Place 52

Chapter 4 To Africa and the First Year
England 56
Hunting Clan 62
Nairobi 63
Shigatini 66
Marangu 69
Martha 74

Chapter 5 Ilboru Years
Ilboru 76
Mama Mesiaki 80
Siafu 85

Patzig 86
Arusha School 88
Shaffer Connection 89
Operation Bootstrap Africa 93

Chapter 6 Years in 'Exile'
The Dismissal.. 96
Loliondo 97
First Walk: Loliondo, Arusha........................... 101
Naomi's Remembrances.................................. 104
Remembrance 107
Father 109

Chapter 7 Two Continents and in Between
Furloughs 112
O'Malley... 123

Chapter 8 Work and Pleasure
Medical.. 126
Theatre... 133
My Direction Connection 136
My Movie Connection 138
Writing Academy 140

Chapter 9 Move to the Hill
A Table Blessed 142
Five Circles of Love 144
Happenings.. 153

Chapter 10 Miracles and Connections
Holy Week 157
Becky 159
Fear 164
The Plane Crash 166

Chapter 11 Assorted Endings
Wittenberg Award 171
Retirement.. 178
The Rest of the Story 180

Chapter 12 People in My Life
Our Kids, Grandkids, and Great-grandkids 187
Missionaries and Mks 197

Appendix: Fruits of the Writing Academy
The Twenty-third Psalm 201
They Come to Our Door 204
Three-Legged Stool 205
Christmas 206
Beautiful Feet 207
Count Your Many Blessings 208
My Backdoor Bench 208
Sunrise Symphony 210
Purple Prelude 211
McAllister Wedding 211

Epilogue 213

Dedication

To my dear and precious
grandchildren and great-grandchildren

As I look into your beautiful faces
and reflect on the wonder in your eyes,
I'm overtaken with gratitude,
for you are the most precious gifts ever given.

As your young lives are being shaped by your "connections,"
I have a desire that your Nana Simonson's story
be one of those connections.

Preface

"How on earth will I ever get to Africa and see the Maasai?" wondered fifteen-year-old Eunice Nordby. The Rev. Richard Reusch, former missionary to the Maasai in Tanganyika, had just taken her hand and said, "You, my child, will one day go to my Maasai."

Eunice's dream was born. Reusch's statement and his stories of the Maasai awakened in her an interest in Africa and, perhaps, medical work among the Maasai. Her mission interest was given a boost when she met and began dating fellow Concordia College student, David Simonson. David had grown up in a parsonage with many visitors who were serving in exciting mission careers. During his first year at the seminary, Simonson also met Dr. Richard Reusch. As a result, David's interest also began to focus on the Maasai.

When David and Eunice married, the Maasai and Tanganyika were a part of their dreams. As David completed his seminary education and Eunice finished nursing school, their anticipation of going to Tanganyika (now Tanzania) grew. What follows is Eunice's autobiography, her account of how she got to the Maasai and of the fifty-five years she and her growing family spent among them.

Introduction

I have been encouraged by so many dear friends to write of my life. I must confess I have not felt I was a noteworthy subject. Jim Klobuchar, who wrote the book, *The Cross Under the Acacia Tree*, encouraged me to prepare a sequel to his book. Without his encouragement and loving help, I never would have started. After waiting for some great bundle of wisdom and skill to drop on me from above to enable me to write, it has finally seeped into this aging brain that all I have accomplished is getting a stiff neck looking for it to drop.

At this time in my life, I find myself thanking God each and every day, not only for the tremendous blessings he has bestowed that have enriched my life, but also the many "connections" and "God-incidents" that have occurred and continue daily, as I meet and talk with people. As I set out to recount my past experiences, many of these connections have become obvious as the segments join and become complete. The continual intertwining of these connections has so intrigued and amazed me that, as I began to write, it was obvious my story would have to be within the context of these connections. The meshing of time, lives, exhilarating experiences, and tragic experiences, together with poems, hymns, and Bible verses connect together to make me who I am.

Acknowledgments

My heartfelt thanks to:

The many who willingly transcribed my hand-written stories into computer files:

Jen Erickson
Serena Simonson
Annette Simonson

Naomi Simonson, who has taken on the greatest bulk of the transcription and editing, gathering photos from family and friends, and working with the publisher

Husband, Dave, who reminded me often to "get it written"

Our gracious Lord, who sustains and blesses

Soli Deo Gloria

CHAPTER ONE

Early Years in North Dakota

Early Childhood

My mother was a petite woman, and my rather large head prevented her from birthing me easily. So, after thirty-six hours of pain, she was taken to St. Joseph's Hospital in Dickinson, North Dakota, where the doctors used something like a big monkey wrench to smoosh my head a bit. (I learned later it was called a retractor, but an uncle who prided himself on his sense of humor, thought "monkey wrench" would fit me better.) As an adult, when I would come up with some bizarre ideas, I would just blame it on the "monkey wrench," although I'd been assured the early procedure was handled by loving, praying hands. The prayers of my mother and father got me safely through the first few days of my life, and I quickly grew strong. My mother was not as fortunate, for after giving birth to my brother,

Mom and Dad holding me

Harold, one year later, she was told that she would not be able to have more children.

My first real childhood memories were from the time I was about three years old. My parents, little brother Harold, and I had to leave North Dakota because my father had nearly died of a ruptured peptic ulcer. (Of course, my medical knowledge at that time did not include words like peptic ulcer.) In my father's weakened state, he was told he should not work, so we moved back to Wisconsin to live among relatives. It was only later that I was told my father could not work during those years, which were some of the toughest for everyone—the Great Depression.

The one room we shared in a tenement building for the unemployed, became the first home of which I have memory. It was very noisy! There were many families living in the building and the walls dividing us were very thin, but there were lots of little ones to play with! We were better off than many, because my mother was a nurse and she found work in the local hospital. I was told my father had to sweep streets in order to maintain our place in this government project.

During this time, there was a dear woman named Mrs. Jones who would look after Harold and me. I remember sitting in her lap while she read *Petunia Brown* to us over and over. It did not take long before I had memorized this book, and I can remember the first time I "read" it to my mother and father. They must have known that I had memorized it, but because I used lots of expression and knew exactly when to turn the pages, their response made me feel so important. From that day on, my desire to read and entertain knew no bounds. As a three year old, I loved amazing visitors by "reading" Petunia Brown.

Thirty-five years later I was speaking in that same city and a lovely older woman came walking toward me, and I cried out, "Mrs. Jones!" She was as amazed at my remembering her as I was of seeing her again. What a deep impression she had made on this three year old!

One experience, during our time in the tenement house, taught me some very valuable lessons about the realities of human nature. Probably when I was little more than a baby myself, my love for babies became very evident. I wanted to hold every baby I saw, and begged incessantly for a baby doll. It was just before Christmas the year I turned four, and my anticipation of wonderful presents was (I am sure) making my parents uneasy.

A dear uncle who seemed to like me "best of all," had heard of my great desire to have a baby doll that could open and shut its eyes, and he chose to fill the Santa Claus role. On Christmas Eve, as I was opening the small gift from my parents (they could not afford much), there was a knock at the door and a jovial Santa arrived! He did sound a bit like my favorite Uncle Evald, but I felt that was merely coincidental, I knew that he had to be the real thing when he handed me this incredibly beautiful baby doll. Her big, blue eyes opened and shut, and her sweet face was the most wondrous thing I had ever seen. What love I felt for her as I wrapped her soft body in the blanket that had come with her. Her arms, legs and face were porcelain and her big blue eyes that opened and closed had long, curly eyelashes. I remember examining each finger and toe (they even had dimples!) and clutching her to my heart, refusing to be separated from her for any reason.

It did not take long before everyone learned of the story of Santa Claus coming only to our room, and all my little friends came to see my precious baby. How I must have gloated over having received this precious gift! Many of the children asked to hold and play with my Suzy, but I would not share her with any of the eager hands that tried to take her from me.

Then the hard lesson came. My mother had decorated a small box with cloth remnants that made pretty sheets, and she had fashioned a pillow. It made a perfect bed for my little one. I had put her down for a nap and ran off to do something; when I returned, my baby was gone! Harold assured me that he had not taken her, and everyone else I asked denied knowing anything. We searched our apartment, the hallway—no Suzy. I became inconsolable when she could not be found. My father eventually found her in the garbage bin, the stuffing from her soft body ripped out, her rosy cheeks rubbed off with turpentine, her beautiful blue eyes gouged out of their sockets.

It was my first traumatic experience with "death," and I still feel the pain. The lesson carefully explained to me by my loving parents was that I had been selfish and should have shared Baby Suzy with those less fortunate. Then perhaps they would not have destroyed what was not theirs. It was a very tough lesson for a little one, but the lesson has always remained with me.

My mother had a cousin, Henry, who in my childhood perspective was taller than my father and even more serious. He had a fancy Ford that was shiny and black with window flaps that could be let down or tied up. One day he took us for a ride. It was unbearably exciting! (I think I wet my panties.) I remember how fun it was to roll the window curtains up and wave to everyone like I was royalty. Uncle Henry must have had money because he had a house that was painted yellow, my favorite color, and it had both an upstairs and a downstairs. So, even though he scared me, I still was very impressed. He must have had a kind heart because he invited us to come live with him for a while. I remember my parents crying because they were so happy to have a home again. To this day, I cry more from happiness and goodness than from sorrow.

My brother and I nearly ruined this happy state for our family. I do not remember the circumstances for our being left alone in Uncle Henry's house—they were never explained to me—but the incident is still very vivid. There was a fine wood-burning stove in the kitchen, with lots of shining chrome on the doors to the firebox and the oven. A large wood box stood next to it, with nicely split pieces of logs stacked inside. Someone had left a large piece of cardboard in the box as well, and Harold and I thought it would be fun to open that shiny firebox door and put the cardboard in. Harold grabbed the cardboard, but when he was unable to completely force it in, he decided to take it out and put it back in the wood box. How quickly that burning piece of cardboard ignited the logs in the box! Flames climbed the wall; smoke filled the room. The next thing I remember was Cousin Henry pulling us out of the burning kitchen, and the great clatter and bells of the fire engine arriving. Some of life's lessons are learned by tough experience, and this was one of those. I did enjoy watching the fire engine though, but not enough to ever want to start another fire.

We had some wonderful grandparents, and time spent with them was always special. My father was a serious man, and his father, Christian O. Nordby, was even more serious. He was a large man with a fierce, black mustache that completely covered his mouth; I wondered if it was designed to hide his smiles. When I was small, my grandpa and his

Nordby farm in rural Baron, Wisconsin Grandpa Christian and Grandma Carrie sitting in rocking chairs on the porch

wife moved into town and lived by the railroad tracks. It was not easy for them to move from the farm. My father's oldest brother inherited the big, beautiful farm outside of town when my grandparents changed homes.

I called my grandpa's wife Grandma Carrie, but I was told she was really my grandpa's third wife. This made me very curious about how the first two had died. (I was never told the circumstances.) Carrie was not very well, so we were always cautioned to be on very good behavior when we were around her. One thing she did that always pleased me was to give us orange juice made from an extract sold by the Watkins traveling salesman. Somehow, I felt this Watkins man must be quite extraordinary to carry around all these "magic" bottles.

I loved going to their house because trains fascinated me. There were many serious lectures and spankings when I would disobey and hide near the tracks to feel the trains go by. An older cousin had told me that if you got too close to the fast motion of the train you could be sucked in, so I would hold on to a tree with all my might and try to feel that force. It seemed I was always discovered by someone before the train passed.

The history of our ancestors is something we all should discover. The hardships they endured in moving from "the old land" (Norway and Sweden) shows what strong, determined, religious, hard-working people they were. It is by their perseverance, that we are what we are today, and many of our blessings are directly influenced by these amazing relatives. Recently, while going through my old journals, I came across a biography of this fierce-looking grandfather of mine, Christian Nordby, who originally came from Gudbrandsdalen, Norway, and settled to farm in Black River Falls, Wisconsin. He arrived in America with just five dollars in his pocket! It is another "connection," because Dave's grandfather also came from Gudbrandsdalen at around the same time in the 1880s. I wonder if they knew each other. To learn that Dave's grandparents and my grandparents were from the same town is an exciting connection.

My mother's parents took care of Harold and me quite often when Mother worked nights at the hospital and Father had speaking assignments in neighboring towns. These were special times for me. Grandpa Gus Benson was a fun, little man who loved to tell stories about his childhood in Sweden. I was espe-

cially excited to be told that he had been "one of the best danc-
ers in Sweden." (My Norwegian relatives would not even talk
about dancing except in terms of condemnation.) I could never
hear music without moving and wiggling about, so I decided I
must be more Swede than Norwegian. Grandpa Gus loved coffee,
and he would hold me in his lap as he was drinking his coffee,
then give me a teaspoon with a sugar lump. I would dip this
gently into his coffee cup and watch the lump suck up the coffee,
then suck the coffee out of the sugar. Yummy!

My sweet, gentle grandmother, Amelia, had her own special
treat for me when I had been very good—graham crackers
broken up into a big glass of cold milk. I really did try to be extra
good for them. Several of my mother's brothers and sisters lived
in the area, and all were so kind to us. I guess everyone was
poor, but we surely never felt that since there was love and we
always felt secure.

When I was five, we moved out to an uncle's farm where
my father worked as a hired man. There was a little neighbor
boy there who played with us. He claimed to love me very much
and told me we would marry when we grew up. He said we could
not kiss until we were grown up, but we could kiss my kitten and
pass it back and forth. It is amazing that poor kitten survived!

The First Parsonage

I loved living in the country, but my parents were finding
life difficult, and I would often see my mother crying. Our
prayers would always include asking God to call Father back into
church work. He had fully recovered and was anxious to serve as
a pastor again. That same year, I remember walking into the
garden and seeing Father holding Mother; they seemed to be
laughing, crying, kissing, and hugging all at the same time.
When they saw me, they pulled me into this embrace and told
me Father had received a call from three rural churches in North
Dakota. There was such excitement as they talked about answered prayer and how great God was. Father would be a full-
time pastor again; we would have a big house of our own; we
would live in the country; we could have cows and chickens and
a big garden. As a grownup, I realized just how deeply my parents had suffered without ever causing concern to us little ones.

Suddenly we had a Chevy, and it was packed for the long trip to Portland, North Dakota. I had just turned six; the thought of a new home, as well as starting school, was bursting my buckles. My unending questions must have driven my parents wild!

How well I remember the arrival at the parsonage! I can still feel the excitement as we drove up the drive to the big house. I wanted to get out of the car and run in to claim and discover. But a group of parishioners were waiting to wel-

My parents with Harold and me

come us, so I was warned to be on "good behavior," and I did want to make a good impression.

The square house, two stories plus attic and basement, was sided with newly-painted, white walls. The spacious front porch stretched across the front of the house, covered in climbing ivy. The ladies had prepared a lovely lunch that they served on this porch. Would we ever get to go inside? My excitement caused an urgency to go potty, so a dear lady took me around to the outhouse that was a short distance from the house. To my delight, there were three holes—one just my size—and I imagined it would have been perfect for Papa Bear, Mama Bear, and Baby Bear.

Finally, the time came to enter this magic house. The front

Our parsonage in rural Portland

entry was large with a stairway going up to the second story. Under the stairs was a large storage closet (just perfect to hide away). One door opened into a formal living room and the other into a large dining room where on one wall hung a telephone—a magical wooden box with a slanting shelf on which one could put a pencil and paper. The receiver hung on the left side and the crank on the right with the speaking cone in front. I would soon learn that each house had its own ring, and that our three long rings would often bring many listeners because the preacher was often called to visit a sick member or put some business on the church calendar. I would also learn that "rubberneckers" could prove to be very embarrassing when boys would begin calling me. Six long cranks was the emergency signal that would bring everyone to their phones. Once a fire alert was given in that manner, and all rushed to the rescue!

But I digress. Beyond the dining room, we entered a large kitchen. I was intrigued by the large wood stove and a sink with a hand pump to bring up water from the cistern. I asked why the kitchen was so big. I was told the former pastor, for whom the house was built, had twelve children, and most of their activities took place in the kitchen. I could imagine how much fun twelve kids would have had here. There were five doors in the kitchen— one to the dining room, one to the basement, another to a pantry, one to a back stairway, and a fifth to an attached closed porch where things were stored.

There was a room off the dining room that Mother and Father chose as their bedroom. I thought it was strange that they would be so far away from the bedrooms that Harold and I would occupy upstairs. Yet, I could hardly wait to go upstairs where I was told I could pick any of the four big bedrooms. We used the front stairway, as the unlit back stairway was not a pleasant place. Later, though, I found the spooky back stairs to be a perfect place to bring friends to tell the many ghost stories I had heard (or made up). We climbed the stairway to a landing with a window, then turned and climbed the remaining steps. A room on the left was divided into a study and a library for the pastor. I choose the first door on the right for my room. It was spacious with a huge closet and a window facing the road. The few clothes I had would be lost in all that space. Harold chose the next room; he wanted to look out on the barn and garden. The two big rooms remaining would be perfect for the games and plays I planned on staging there. Oh, it was so thrilling!

"Would you like to see the attic?" I was the only one who wanted to explore every nook and cranny, so I was told this could wait until later. (I loved the attic with its two window cupolas.)

There must have been furniture, but all I remember was the joy of having our very own house with rooms and spaces for us to occupy. The spaces outside were wonderful too: a small barn where we later kept a cow and many chickens, a garage with a tool shed behind, a wood shed, and, of course, the three-holer.

We had a large lawn bordered by a windbreak on the north, because winters are fierce in North Dakota. A row of lilac bushes divided our lawn from the dusty gravel road east of the house. When I learned to tell directions, I always thought of the road because it ran north and south. North Dakota is measured out in one-mile squares—so handy to know where you are going and how far you have gone.

At the time of our move, North Dakota was just beginning to recover from the terrible years of drought and depression, but dust storms still took place, with black drifts and tumbleweeds everywhere. Our wonderful house was well-built, but after every dust storm it was my job to dust and sweep. The wet rags my mother had placed in every window sill became sodden with mud. Among my least favorite memories of that wonderful house are of dusting and doing the dishes.

This would be our home for twenty years, and each part of it holds unique memories for me.

Primrose # 2

As a child in rural North Dakota, my social life centered not only on my father's parishes, but also on the country school known as Primrose #2. At the time I began attending, the building was very state of the art. It was a simple, square, wooden

Primrose #2 school house in rural Portland

Classroom Primrose #2

structure painted white, with a basement that provided a warm place to play at recess when temperatures kept us from going outside, and two cloakrooms—one for the boys and one for the girls—each boasting coat hooks, shelves for lunch pails, and even flushing chemical toilets. The one large classroom contained rows of metal-framed desks with wooden seats and tops that had grooved slots for our pencils and holes to accommodate our inkwells. Shelves under the top of the desk provided a space in which we could slide our books. All the desks faced the teacher, who would call us up to her desk, a grade at a time, to recite our lessons. On the east side of the building many large windows looked out over the school grounds where we played at recess and a grove of cottonwood trees near the road.

Perhaps what I loved most about that building was the raised platform, two steps up, at the rear of the large room. That platform served as our stage whenever we put on special programs. I especially loved preparing for our Christmas programs. My enthusiasm for storytelling and acting found an outlet during those times. While family members described me as "sturdy" and "tough," in my mind I was beautiful and petite on stage. Teachers encouraged my artistic abilities and had me create background scenes on the blackboard mounted on the wall behind the stage. I felt very proud to be chosen to design murals to enhance the plays we performed.

Our performances were very basic. We had no piano to provide accompaniment, but that did not matter because the programs seemed magical to me. Black curtains separated us from the audience, and I remember what a thrill it was to finally be old enough to be a curtain puller. Whether the teachers enjoyed my participation or whether they wanted me to "hush up" and stop bugging them, I had many opportunities to show off by being in plays, reciting poems, and presenting readings.

Each year, we had a huge Christmas tree mounted on the main floor below the stage. We students decorated the tree with homemade paper chains and other constructed baubles. For lights on the tree, we had little clip-on candle holders that held lighted candles during our program. That was long before fire marshals forbade that sort of thing, and I must admit we had our share of paper chain fires. Each year, we also made a huge star that would hang from the ceiling.

After our Christmas programs, we students were treated to paper bags filled with peanuts, an apple or orange if available, and those amazing chocolate mound candies filled with a white confection. As I remember, the filling really had no flavor except for sweet. That did not matter, because I loved them. I ate everything else first, making sure no one else could get at my treasures before I slowly savored those few candies one by one.

The mothers of the district always provided a wonderful lunch after our programs. I remember the smell of egg coffee (an old Scandinavian tradition of mixing a raw egg with the coffee grounds) making me feel especially warm and contented, even though the taste of it was awful (unless taken with lots of cream and sugar). When I smelled that coffee, I knew it would be accompanied by open-faced sandwiches and very often my favorite dessert: spice cake with penuche frosting. As we ate, there was always laughter and conversation among the adults, while we children played together, being the typical kids we were. It was a simple time, but those memories still warm my heart.

Since we were the preacher's kids and because my father was a very serious and proper preacher, we never stayed at evening school events past his closing prayer and benediction. We were always the first to leave. I knew there must be more to these outings, but investigating my theory seemed beyond my control. Curiosity won out the evening I decided to deliberately leave my sweater behind. After the prayer and benediction, my father loaded us up in the Chevy. We were almost home when I made my move. I moaned, "Oh, dear! I forgot my sweater!" I must admit, my father was not very happy with me, but he did turn around and head back to the school so that I could retrieve it. As I walked toward the school, feeling quite proud of the deception, I heard music and then I saw everyone dancing and having a wonderful time. I knew it! I just knew there were more to those evenings than what we were allowed to witness! I thought it was totally unfair that we could not participate!

Primrose #2 was located a mile and a quarter from the parsonage. My brother, Harold, and I walked that distance every school day, rain or shine, snow or sleet, hot or cold, in sickness and in health. Looking back, it truly was a beautiful and picturesque route that took us down to the bank of the Goose River, then over the bridge, around Gus Gilbertson's pasture, and up the road near the farm of my friend Dolores, before finally arriving at the school grounds.

Each season provided us with delicious sights and smells that sparked our young minds and piqued our interest in God's creation. When school started in the fall, the mornings were crisp, dewy, filled with the smells of fertile earth being readied for winter, combined with the aromas of overripe fruit and the last cutting of hay. On hot walks home, bugs would cluster and swarm atop weeds giving up their seeds to the earth. The crunch of the dry dust beneath our feet and the heat waves on the horizon actually made us long for the first snow. Along the river there was a grove of chokecherry trees with fruit we always hoped we would get before the birds did. When the clusters were

Harold in me in our snowsuits

ripe, we would pull handfuls of them off the branches and put them in our mouths. Their alum-like tartness would pucker our faces, and we would laugh at all our contortions. I have always thought that "chokecherry" was such an appropriate name for that berry.

In the winter, when the snows were deep and the winds cuttingly vicious, Harold and I would ski to school. Most people do not realize that North Dakota developed good skiers, but I assure you, Harold and I had to be pretty good to be able to handle that steep valley embankment without falling before we got to the bridge to cross the river. My parents were especially worried about Harold during this time. As they helped us into our coats, boots, and the many layers of scarves they made us wear, my father would say to me, "Now Eunice, I want you to watch out for your brother so that he doesn't fall asleep in the snow." Of course, being the dutiful big sister, I would look into my father's eyes to assure him that I would indeed watch over Harold to make sure he would not be tempted to lie down and go to sleep in the snow. I always thought that it was a strange request. Who in their right mind would want to lie down and sleep in the snow? It was bitterly cold!

One of my favorite activities during the winter was walking to the river to clear the snow off areas of ice, clamp skate-runners to the bottoms of my boots, and pretend I was Sonja Henie, performing Olympics-worthy pirouettes and double axels. Even though I ended up falling flat on my face many times, it did not bother me in the least because I would land with arms gracefully outstretched. I was sure I convinced those with me that it was planned and done on purpose.

In the spring, our area came alive with the activity of farmers preparing their fields for planting. On my way to school, I loved walking amid the new plant growth and watching the birds building their nests. The spring rains caused the river to swell, and it was amazing to watch it come alive with fish traveling upstream to spawn.

Now, I cannot recall the specific reason, but I remember being in a tremendous hurry to get to school one glorious spring morning. We had to walk around Gus Gilbertson's pasture because his property line followed the bend in the river. Gus Gilbertson owned a bull—and not just any bull, but a mean, vicious Hereford with a reputation known throughout the township. I was so afraid of that bull, that I had not been tempted to even consider the possibility of taking the shortcut through Gus Gilbertson's pasture. That is, until that spring morning.

My heart was pounding as I surveyed the pasture; there was no bull in sight. I crawled under the barbed-wire fence and hurriedly made my way toward the school. I did not want to jinx my good luck by looking around too much. Suddenly, I felt the ground shake and heard the sound of hooves galloping behind me. As I turned, I saw the dust rising from the cow path on which I was walking. That nasty, old bull was heading straight for me!

I took off like a shot and made a beeline toward the fence, sliding under the barbed-wire just as the bull was close enough to do some serious damage. Flushed and shaken, I brushed the dust from my frock, pulled the weeds from my hair and leggings, and marched toward the school. Yes, that was one mean and nasty old bull!

On any given year, there were about fifteen students at Primrose #2, but in the eight years I attended, I never had a classmate (in the same grade). It was never a hardship though because we all played together, making up games and amusing ourselves during recess. One game I especially loved to play was Nib. It was a creative game we made up with the objective of becoming the "nibber." The nibber would set a piece of wood about nine inches long (the nib) across a small trench we had dug. The nibber would then use a long nibbing stick to go under the wood in the trench and flip the nib to one of the waiting participants. If you caught the nib or if you picked the nib up and threw it, hitting the nibbing stick, you earned the opportunity of being the next nibber. While my description may sound a bit confusing, I assure you the game was great fun and only one of the many games we made up. However, Nib was replaced by softball when one of our teachers purchased a ball and bat for the school. I loved to play softball!

We used to have an annual Sport Day at Primrose #2. Students at all the schools in the township competed in events that included not only long jump, high jump, running races, and other physical competitions, but also speech events such as declamation. As I remember, I was pretty good at some of the physical events, but I was *great* at declamation. I won every year. I remember this one year especially well. My father had given me a quarter for our school outing to Finley, North Dakota, where the schools were to meet for Sport Day. As I looked out the window of the bus as we drove into town, I noticed that Finley had a movie theater. I had never been to a movie theater or seen a movie for that matter, so it became a real Kodak moment for me. I participated in all my athletic events, and won the declamation contest (albeit without my teacher's help, as she was too interested in the gentlemen seated around her—but that is another story). I must have had some time on my hands, and I was thinking of that movie theater and the twenty-five cents were burning a hole in my pocket. Finley was a very small town, so walking to the the-ater was not at all difficult for me, nor was purchasing a ticket and those *two* ice cream cones. I saw an Abbot and Costello movie, and had an absolutely glorious time all by myself. It never occurred to me that while I was enjoying the movie, the teachers and other students were frantically looking for me. When I returned to the athletic field, still licking the sticky ice cream off my fingers, I found that several people were *very* upset with me—and that was even before my parents knew what I had done.

As a child I loved scary stories. I loved to hear them, and I loved to make them up. Beyond Gus Gilbertson's pasture was an abandoned and dilapidated old farmhouse that I was sure was haunted. As I remember, it was set back from the road and surrounded by untamed weeds and half-dead trees which produced eerie shadows across its worn, unpainted exterior and cracked, broken windows, even during the middle of the day. I conjured many tales in my mind about that house: from buried treasure and pirate booty (although North Dakota did not see too many pirates), to it being full of dead bodies that turned into zombies at night. More than anything, I wanted to explore that old place, but I just did not dare go alone. I finally convinced my friend, Dolores, to accompany me. As we walked through the tall, gnarled weeds to the front door barely on its hinges, I suddenly did not feel nearly as confident as when I first imagined this adventure. I told Dolores that she could go in first if she wanted, but she quickly told me that this was my big idea. So, I had to be the brave one after all. I slowly pushed in the door, and the movement loosened dirt and cobwebs that peppered our hair. We would have laughed at how we looked if we had not been so scared. Slowly, hand in hand, we crept into the front room.

While I was prepared for something to suddenly jump out and attack us, we only found dirt and clutter. We relaxed a bit and began to look through all the paraphernalia that had been left by the last inhabitants: old books, rickety furniture. We began to feel like fortune hunters. The floors were rotted out in areas, so we carefully watched where we stepped as we made our way further into the house. Soon we not only felt comfortable, we felt like the greatest adventurers in the world! As we continued our exploration, we talked about how much fun we were having. Soon we were planning other excursions to uninhabited farmsteads. We could form a club and finance it with all the treasures we would find! The possibilities were endless.

That was when we heard it—from out of nowhere, the repeated clacking of a stick being drawn down the siding on the outside of the house. Up, then down. Up, then down. Rapidly, then slowly and rhythmically. Dolores and I did not waste any time trying to figure out who or why. We just tore out of there as fast as we could. We bolted out of the yard, out of the driveway, and down the road, praying for speed and safety (and perhaps a little forgiveness) along the way. When we could run no farther, we stopped and put our hands on our knees, panting, slowly regained our breath. We looked at each other, speechless, not knowing what had just occurred. But we knew we were not going back there again. That place *was* haunted!

As we continued our walk home, Dolores very thoughtfully and deliberately confided that her parents might not want her being part of an adventurer's club, but that she would not feel badly if I decided I needed to get another friend with whom to start the club. I put my arm around her shoulders and assured her that she was my best friend in the whole wide world and that I would never want to be in a club without her. We could just forget it!

We learned, much later, that Dolores' father had been collecting wood outside that old house and was fully aware of what we were doing. He had timed his trickery to have its greatest effect.

Bobby was a good friend to me all through my years at Primrose #2. Bobby was short and pudgy, as I remember, but he had amazingly thick, curly, blonde hair and the most beautiful sky-blue eyes. I was often teased that Bobby was my boyfriend, but he was more like my partner in crime. He may have resembled a cherub, but Bobby was no angel. If there was a possibility for mischief, Bobby was leading the pack.

I must stop here and philosophize a bit. I believe God gave each one of us a childhood, so that we could utilize our imaginations, our creativity, and occasionally be led astray—"kids will be kids." As a preacher's kid, I was constantly reminded that everyone was watching me, so I had better be as close to perfect as possible. I was not perfect, nor did I care to be. However, I loved my parents and enjoyed those around me, so I always tried my best to behave so I would be thought of in a kindly manner and considered to be a good girl. That being said, I will continue my story.

During the long, hot days of summer, the Goose River made the best backdrop for any game of fantasy, and several of us would make a point of meeting daily where the river made a bend and the heavily-leafed trees provided a cooling shade. We would swim, play cowboys and Indians, make up games, or simply talk together and explore.

One day only Bobby and I were at the river, catching frogs. There is a real talent to catching frogs. One must be quiet and stealthy on the approach, then quick to grab from both the frog's front and back, or they will simply leap away. Bobby was much better at it than I was, so I mostly splashed around and made mud pies. Soon, I noticed that Bobby had grabbed an oat straw from a nearby field and was intent on a project. I, the curious one, ran through the water to the bank where he was sitting. He explained that he was helping the frogs swim faster. He inserted the straw into the frog's butt, then blew through it to inflate the frog full of air. I watched, mesmerized, as he released the bloated frog into the water. The escaping air jetted the frog out into deeper water so quickly it caused a wake in its path. We giggled at the thought of a frog passing gas. I quickly found my own straw and set out to get another frog. It took a while, but I was determined to help a frog swim faster, too. I finally caught a big, old, fat frog, too slow to escape my inexperienced hands. Bobby helped me insert the straw, and I proceeded to blow. It was not as easy as Bobby had made it look, and I am sure I looked a bit like Dizzy Gillespie blowing his trumpet, with my cheeks all puffed out and my face turning as red as my hair. I soon felt I had achieved some success, but after I put the frog in the water, the angle of its legs caused it to go in all directions—like when you release an inflated balloon. For some reason, after watching that poor old frog, I did not feel like doing it again, and I told Bobby so. Bobby muttered something like, "Girls!" Years later, during my nursing training, it made me smile when I learned what was necessary in the process of doing a colonoscopy. Yes, one must get inflated with air.

I can't say I was a fashion plate when I attended Primrose #2, but I was always clean, comfortable, and appropriate in what I wore. Most of my clothes were hand-me-downs, given to me from my father's parishioners and carefully remade by my mother on her Singer treadle sewing machine. I never even thought about clothes in one way or another, as long as I was covered. I'm sure part of the reason I was protected from the need to have the latest fashions was that we lived in rural North Dakota. I was not exactly bombarded with fashion media. My father allowed only two magazines into our house: *The Lutheran Standard* and the *National Geographic*. I loved reading about all the exotic places in the *National Geographic,* and I remember thinking how amazing it would be to be able to travel or live in areas where the cultures were so different—it seemed a pipe dream. Yes, I enjoyed the *National Geographic*, *The Lutheran Standard*, too. But they did not exactly offer beauty tips or show off the latest styles.

My attitude changed the day my mother brought home a brand new, store-bought dress of dark green taffeta with a short-sleeved shirtwaist bodice, a white Peter Pan collar, and a circular skirt on which were appliquéd an apple and the words "An apple for the teacher" on its lower front. It was beautiful, it fit me perfectly, and it was mine. My mother smiled at how happy I was, but let me know that it was a thoughtful parishioner who had bought the dress and that I must let them know how thankful I was for their kind generosity.

As a child, winter was a wonderland, just like the song in many ways. Snow seemed to make everything clean. The air was fresh and crisp; the dusty, drying grass was covered; the crystal icing on the leafless branches looked like magic wands. The games and other activities were such fun. Even skiing to school was a challenge that I enjoyed, though it was often difficult after a heavy snow. Harold and I followed in the tracks made by our teacher, which displeased her very much as we often messed them up with our little skis and occasional tumbles.

Tobogganing became a real thrill when our neighborhood received a four-passenger sled for Christmas. The speed with which we descended our steep hill was thrilling. We were so thankful for our neighbor's generous sharing. Cups of hot cocoa and cookies were shared in our big, warm kitchen after these adventures.

Skating was always a favorite activity for me, with my grand dreams of being another Sonja Henie (not very easy on my old pair of clamp-on blades). Skating parties on a bigger pond than our little Goose River were a source of much fun.

At Christmas time, the Norwegian community had a social activity much like Halloween trick-or-treat. It was called Yuleboking. I have asked other Norwegians if they ever had done this, but no one else has never heard of it. So, it was unique for this community and enjoyed by all. Groups of six to eight younger and older adults would disguise themselves and go from farm to farm. Much laughter and false voices made the identifying difficult, until one had been named. After the first person had been identified, the rest were more easily named, as everyone knew from what family or group they came. Masks then were removed, and a treat of hot cocoa or cider with some Christmas baked goods was shared. Then they were off to the next farm. As a six-year-old, these people scared me until I saw the familiar faces, which were so cheery and loving.

By my third Christmas in North Dakota, I begged my parents to let me be in one of these groups. "Too young," was the response, but I never gave up easily. My parents gave up, and they agreed that Harold and I could dress up and go across the road to our teacher's house. With lots of padding and funny masks (where my mother found them, I never asked), we trundled over to the nearby house. After imitating the cheerful grown-up, "Ho ho ho, Merry Christmas!" we were ushered into the cozy kitchen, and our teacher and her husband welcomed us with words like, "Where did they come from?" Of course, they knew who we were, but they played along until I got the giggles. It was such fun, but in my mirth I backed up to lean against a wall. Being unable to see through my mask, I leaned against the open door to the pantry and landed in an open crock of buttermilk! My great adventure met a soggy end.

As a teenager, I joined my peer group and enjoyed a more dignified experience. That is, until I once put on Father's boots with blocks inside to give me height, an old sheepskin coat with pillows inside to give me girth, and an old, fur-lined cap. Scarves across my face completed my ugly disguise. At one farm my false voice and appearance fooled a couple of farm hands, who thought I was one of their drinking buddies, and they started to tell me a dirty story. I pulled away, and when others identified me, these poor men were mortified—the *preacher's* daughter!

Let the Beauty

Being an adolescent and feeling ugly was just plain painful. My red hair was not my only deficit. Steel-rimmed glasses gave my round face an owlish look. Adding to these problems, my skin was covered with freckles!

These freckles were not cute little spots that "sprinkled" dainty noses. Oh, no, these spots covered every area of my skin the sun touched. My saintly mother tried to comfort me by calling them "angel kisses." She encouraged me to stay out of the sun, but that was like telling a bird not to fly. I tried lemon juice and even attempted bleach, all to no avail. My futile attempts only gave me a rash.

The neighbor's good-looking hired man teased me unmercifully. "You been chasing the manure spreader again?" was one of his favorite lines. Oh, how this hurt!

Then one day a marvelous thing happened.

My father had invited a visiting missionary to stay with us for the week of mission emphasis. Cora was a woman of warmth and understanding. Her stories of Christ's work in far-off places captivated me. I felt a strong desire to be like her, to go to Africa with God's love.

Cora knew I enjoyed playing piano and invited me to play duets with her. One day, as we were laughing and playing together, she looked at me and stopped playing. She took my hands in hers, looking deeply into my eyes. My heart nearly stopped as she paused. She then said words that changed me, "My dear, you have the most radiant skin." She continued, "The love of Jesus just shines in your face."

I did not suddenly *like* my freckles, but the sense of despair over "looks" was lifted. The promise that God could use me to shine for him gave me the assurance and confidence I needed.

Even now, after fifty-four years as a missionary in Africa, I recall that event. "Let the beauty of Jesus be seen in me" became my song, thanks to Cora.

Death of a Friend

"School is out for today, children, but you must stay here until the storm passes," our vacation Bible school teacher told us. Summer storms could be wild and severe in North Dakota, so we did not argue, but gathered at the window of our country school house to watch the fireworks. They were indeed spectacular. We would watch the flash and then begin to slowly count: Ten . . . twenty . . . thirty . . . forty . . . fifty . . . until the rumble and crash came. We felt so smart and secure knowing from our count that the storm was quite a distance away from us.

My dear friend, Delores, had invited me to spend the afternoon with her at their house, just a quarter mile from the school. (I lived one more mile beyond that.) My father had agreed, but with the admonition not to stay for supper, as he did not want me to be a burden on that poor family. I loved Delores' mom, but was a bit frightened of her father, who could be quite fierce, especially if he had been drinking. Delores and I hoped the storm would pass quickly so we could play.

It seemed only a few minutes before the flash and the crash were simultaneous, and we were nearly thrown to the floor when a bolt struck on the road just outside the school. We screamed and held on to each other. "I sure hope nobody was out there!" I said to Delores.

The storm moved on, and we picked up our lunch boxes and headed to Delores' home. As we splashed through the puddles on our muddy road, we noticed my brother taking a detour into the adjacent field, avoiding something in the road. This puzzled us, until we approached and saw the bottoms of two boots and what looked like a man. Terrified, we ran the few hundred feet to the house and called Delores' mom.

She came smiling and asked, "Did Dad reach the school to walk you home? He has been looking forward to your coming so much." The horror on our faces stopped her, and she asked, "What has happened?" Delores sobbed, "I think Dad is lying in the road!" We returned to the lifeless form of the man, the husband, the father. The moments that followed changed much in my thinking and my life. As I watched, my friend stood helplessly as her mother lay in the mud near her husband, frantically trying to breathe life into his burned body.

This was my first encounter with real death and witnessing the inexpressible anguish of those whom I loved. I knew shame for having judged a man unjustly. I now knew a bit more about life and death.

In Winter I Get Up By Night

In winter I get up by night

And dress by yellow candle-light.

These words, from the poem by Robert Louis Stevenson, always described my feelings of winter mornings when Mother would come in with a lighted candle to wake me. When she was assured I was awake, she would move on to wake Harold.

As I struggled to pull on my hateful winter underwear, I could hear my father in the dining room below tuning in "The First News Analysis of the Day by Alex Dryer for Skelly Oil." He would then add lignite coal to the potbelly stove. By the time I was dressed, Mother had cooked oatmeal for our breakfast. Only in later years did I ever reflect on the diligence of Mother and Father, as they needed to prepare the fire in the wood stove to have everything ready.

In summer quite the other way,

I have to go to bed by day.

The wonders of summer were ushered in by the beauty of spring—lilacs and peonies are the fragrance and color that come to mind. We packed away the heavy and burdensome clothes of winter, to don cotton and light fabric. Vacation Bible school changed the curriculum from reading, writing, and arithmetic to stories, hymns, and Jesus. Longer days gave time to enjoy all those wonders and activities.

Father took a few weeks leave and we were packed into the Chevy, headed to Wisconsin for family reunions, picnics, and catching up on everyone's activities there. One special memory was of nights beside Rice Lake, where we had a picnic and boat rides, accompanied by the music of the local band in the bandstand in the park.

As I became a teenager, the experience of Bible camp became a time of spiritual and social growth. Father was dean of boys, and the father of my friend, Chris, was camp dean of Red Willow Lake Bible Camp. We had amazing leadership and speakers who inspired me and led me to a deeper commitment— "Living for Jesus, a life that is true, striving to please him in all that I do. Pledging allegiance, glad-hearted and free, this is the pathway of blessing for me."

Bang, Perry, and Sherbrook

While this title may look like the name of an exclusive New York law firm, in fact, those were the names of my father's parishes outside Portland, North Dakota. Bang (pronounced "bung') was the oldest and largest of the three, with Perry the second and Sherbrook the newest and smallest.

All three churches were wooden structures with steeples pointing heavenward and were within a six-mile radius from the parsonage. Keeping up with the preaching, teaching, and visiting all the parishioners, kept my father on the road quite a lot—going in all directions. His driving was a source of amusement to many, but it was of concern for those of us who often were with him. He drove fast on these narrow, steeply ditched, gravel roads. He had several accidents that nearly took his life and ours.

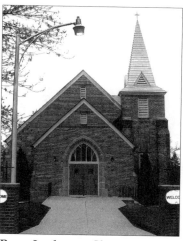

Bang Lutheran Church, rural Portland

There were approximately twenty to thirty families in each congregation. In those days families were very large, so there were lots of people to attend to during the week. Many parishioners, combined with three services each Sunday, kept my father more than busy. Harold and I were required to attend two of these services each Sunday. On the rare Sunday mornings when we were running late, my father would sit in the Chevy and honk the horn until we had make a mad dash to the car. I remember one Sunday morning when our mother had not had time to braid and coil her hair, and we watched as she ran to the car with her waist-length hair flowing behind her. She was beautiful. Of course, it was braided and in place around her head like a halo before she stepped into the church and took her place at the organ.

The wonderful people of Bang, Perry, and Sherbrook were all farmers, some more affluent than others, but all basically struggling. I felt we must be among the richest because we had a large house, a cow, chickens, and the Chevy. The fact that we only wore hand-me-down clothes or made do with the gifts from others never registered with me. On Christmas and Easter a special thanks offering for the pastor was placed on the altar. Father let Harold and me have the pennies (and there were quite a few). We felt like royalty as we stacked them in piles of ten-one offering we nearly made fifty cents each! These dear people would also bring us meat when they butchered. If there was more than we could eat, Mother would can the rest. From Father's garden came much to can or be stored in our cool cellar. We had no refrigeration until I went to high school. What a change the Rural Electric Association (REA) made in our lives!

Confirmation day with Harold and me standing on either side of Pastor Nordby (Dad)

While there were three separate congregations, we all shared and attended many social events like weddings, funerals, circles; all the youth attended one Luther League group. Actually, whole families attended, but it was run by the youth. I loved Luther League because it provided an opportunity for the young people of the church to test their organizational skills as well as provide a venue for us to socialize. Luther League was held every Sunday afternoon in a large, separate building on the Bang campus, utilized for many community events. A typical program consisted of Bible readings and lots of music. There was a women's trio that sang beautifully, and Harold and I often sang together. I remember the song, "Jerusalem," as one we especially enjoyed. After the program, the ladies would serve tasty treats. We would always have activities after our lunch. Rosie would accompany us on the piano while we played circle games such as "The Farmer in the Dell," "Bingo," and "Four in a Boat," but we always ended the evening with the Grand March. It was a super day when I reached the age when I could march! I later learned that what we had been doing was square dancing, but my father would not allow that word ("dance") to be used for one of our activities. It was here that I measured my development from wide-eyed child to an involved and responsible leader in my teens.

The First Call

A wedding! As a fifteen-year-old romantic, I was very excited about the invitation we received. My uncle, John Benson, who had been a widower for many years, was to marry Ruth Bonander, a fine woman, and we were to attend at Braham, Minnesota. All the aunts, uncles and cousins would be there—just one more reason to be excited. My mother had four brothers and three sisters so there were lots of cousins, many of them my age.

I remember very little of the actual wedding, but the reception after the ceremony was very memorable for me as I met one of the most interesting men ever to enter my life. Richard Reusch was the husband of the bride's sister. He and his wife came from Tanganyika where they had met and married while she was serving as a missionary. He had come from Russia—a "White Russian" I was told—who was short of stature but had

Richard Reusch

immense shoulders. He looked like my idea of Agatha Christie's Hercule Poirot with his shiny, bald head, penetrating black eyes, and spectacular black mustache. When we were introduced, he clicked his heels, bent from his waist, and kissed my hand. It was such a dramatic and exciting experience that my heart rate went wild. I thought this only happened in books—this amazing man had just kissed my hand! Wow!

As we cousins were catching up on all that had happened since we had last been together, Dr. Reusch came to me and asked if I would like to see some artifacts he had brought from Tanganyika. What an honor to be chosen by this man to learn something about Africa, a place that had always intrigued me! I had studied articles on Africa in the *National Geographic,* and I already felt a strong pull towards its people.

We went into the church study where he had laid out many things from his beloved Maasai. It was the first time I had heard of the Maasai and, as he shared his deep love for these people with whom he had lived and worked, I was deeply moved. The beads the women made into necklaces and belts, the ebony sticks given to honored elders, a huge shield made of buffalo hide and painted in fascinating patterns with red ocher, white lime and black ash, and a traditional Maasai spear—what treasures, and with each a story. I had never been so intrigued before and felt such a tie to these beautiful, nomadic people. As I sat in awe, Dr. Reusch became very quiet. He reached across the desk and grasped my hands, his penetrating black eyes bore into mine as he said, "You, my child, will one day go to my Maasai."

Side note: If you want to read more about the life of this fascinating man, Dr. Richard Reusch, read *Loyalty*, written by Daniel Johnson and available through The Book Mark at Gustavus Adolphus College, St. Peter, Minnesota (www.richardreusch.com).

Chapter Two

Years of Education

Oak Grove

When the time came for us country kids to begin high school, we needed to arrange for housing in town. No buses or travel pools existed for daily transport. I just assumed my parents would ask Pastor Rotto, father of my friend, Chris, if I could stay there with their nine children. My parents had other plans: I would go to Oak Grove Lutheran High School, a boarding school in Fargo, North Dakota, some sixty miles from home. It is a Christian school with so many opportunities.

Oak Grove Lutheran High School in Fargo, North Dakota

"Why?" My first uncharitable thought was that they did not trust me in the "worldly" environs of town. Was I apt to stray? The reminder came as I thought on Father's teaching: "Put the most charitable construction on all that they do." Of course, they wanted something special for me, and Oak Grove would offer that to me.

I did, however, feel a sense of betrayal for my country kin; I was concerned that they might feel I thought myself better than them. They never showed any of those feelings and, with time, I knew this was a gift of such great blessing for those formative years of my life.

Oak Grove—so aptly named after the lovely park where it was located along the Red River which separated North Dakota from Minnesota—consisted of one huge, long, brick building with a chapel at one end, administration and business offices in the middle, and classrooms on the opposite end. The second story housed the library and the girls' dorm. I was lucky enough to have Kitty Thorsgaard as my roommate the whole time I attended Oak Grove. Kitty was the brightest person in the school and, while she was a year ahead of me, we became the best of friends. Our room was directly across from the library, which gave us great access to knowing who was studying and when.

Kathryn "Kitty" and me at Oak Grove

One day a group of boys saw us through our open door and decided to come to our room and chat. Of course, this was strictly forbidden, but we really could not see the harm. While they were in our room, we saw our housemother, Ms. Jackson, heading for our room. Now, while we did not see the harm in having boys in our room, we also did not want to get into trouble, so we made the boys hide in our closet and under the beds. What made Ms. Jackson suddenly so friendly as to come in, sit down and make small talk, I will never know, but it seemed like it took forever before she decided to leave. We found out later that she was fully aware of everything that was going on and took enjoyment in how uncomfortable she was making everyone. We were very happy that she chose to keep it her little secret, and we chose to talk to boys outside our room from that day on.

I continued to study piano at Oak Grove. When I was very young I began playing songs on the piano by ear. First my mother helped encourage my love for the piano, then my instruction was given over to Rosie who gave me lessons until I went off to Oak Grove. Unfortunately, my favorite musical memory from that period was not my magnificent playing, but rather the dress I wore as a sophomore to my piano recital. It was white chiffon with puffy sleeves, a peasant neckline, and a long, full skirt with a black lace cummerbund. It was beautiful, and I couldn't believe how fortunate I was to receive such a gift: That dress was purchased for me by the same benefactors that had given me that first green store-bought dress years before.

When I became an upperclassman, I got part-time jobs that provided a little spending money for purchasing clothes, school supplies, and a few extras. One job that was sort of fun was working at a drugstore soda fountain. I say it was "sort of" fun

Oak Grove band with me standing in the center holding the big drum

because, while I really enjoyed making sodas, malts, cones, and banana splits, I didn't enjoy squeezing the oranges for the specialty of the house, freshly-squeezed orange juice. There was one particular day that a young gentleman came in and ordered glass after glass after glass of orange juice. After a time I had to comment that he certainly loved his orange juice! "Not particularly, I just really enjoy watching you squeeze the oranges," he replied.

I also worked waiting tables at a hotel restaurant. While I really appreciated the money, it made me realize that I did not want to do that for the rest of my life.

I enjoyed Oak Grove so much that you'd think I would have wanted to stay there longer rather than cut the experience short, but I completed all my requirements in three years, except for one class, which kept me there the first semester of my fourth year. The easy academic load made it very convenient for me to participate in even *more* extracurricular activities. During my junior year, Oak Grove built a new gymnasium that housed all kinds of events that were not only special, but were also "firsts" for the school. The school started a pep band to support its athletic teams, and while piano was my instrument, I found I could play the drums pretty well. Oak Grove put on its first play, "Huckleberry Finn" with me playing one of the leading parts, Becky Thatcher. As art editor of the *Oak Leaves* magazine, I drew the entrance of the new gym for the cover of the magazine, to commemorate its opening. Oh, yes, it was a magical time, but what really put the frosting on the cake was when my friends Shirley and Marlys, a I (a blonde, brunette, and redhead) were chosen as the first Homecoming royalty in Oak Grove history. We were interviewed on the WDAY radio station and the *Fargo Forum* printed an article on the big event. For all these things to happen to a country girl from Portland, North Dakota, seemed almost too good to be true. I was truly thankful.

After these three and a half years at Oak Grove, I moved from Fargo, North Dakota, across the Red River to Concordia College in Moorhead, Minnesota. Starting college a semester earlier than others in my graduating class had its advantages but also some drawbacks: Other freshmen at Concordia were already acclimated and I was the "new girl" who had to fit in. It did not take me long though; I was already accustomed to living away from home, and my new roommate was very welcoming. What was complicated about that first semester was that I was still participating in senior activities at Oak Grove. It was that semester I played Becky in "Huckleberry Finn," which made it

Family photo on my graduation from Oak Grove

necessary to spend many evenings a week at rehearsal at Oak Grove until our show date in February. My Oak Grove boyfriend would get me for rehearsal, but he could not take me back to Concordia because of his 10:00 p.m. curfew. Luckily for me, I met a new friend, who was more than willing to pick me up from Oak Grove and return me to Concordia. I graduated that spring from Oak Grove, plus I had a semester of college credits on my transcript.

Concordia Connection

Concordia had many wonderful teachers, and I thrived on all I was taught. I felt a strong desire to enter the pre-med program, so beside all the 101 requirements, I took several science electives. English and sciences were among my favorites, but chemistry was tough. I would like to think it was difficult for me because the instructor was hard to understand. More likely it was because I was often tempted to skip class and be with the handsome young man who would call me out of class. This handsome man became the big connection in God's plan for my life.

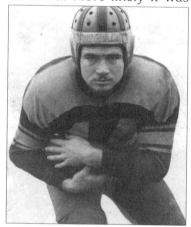

Dave—football captain and fullback for Concordia College, Moorhead, Minnesota

I had admired J. David Simonson that first semester, from the window of my dorm room which overlooked the athletic area where he worked out with fellow football players. What a hunk! I could not believe my good fortune when we were scheduled into the same biology lab, where I found he also was pre-med. I will never forget the day we were required to dissect a frog, a task I found very distasteful. As I was looking at the frog, I realized Dave was watching me. He offered to help do the dirty work, and I was impressed and thrilled—and a bit relieved.

Since I was already dating someone, Dave did not ask me out, but he made me very aware of his interest. Dave's roommates were two gentlemen from my hometown of Portland,

North Dakota. Ken was a very good friend from early childhood and Marlow was the boyfriend of my best friend, Chris, giving me great opportunity to keep track of Dave's whereabouts, should I want to take advantage of his interest.

The summer of 1948 was the beginning for J. David Simonson and me. Our churches were having their annual picnic and program. I was playing the piano which had been hoisted onto the back of a truck for ease of transporting to the picnic grounds. My great surprise came when I looked up from my music and spotted Dave with Ken and Marlow. It is amazing what a person remembers, but Dave was wearing a knit shirt that enhanced his muscular build, and he walked with the confidence befitting royalty. I found it rather difficult playing "I'd Rather Have Jesus" when my mind was on this breathtaking sight. I am just glad my hands could continue as my mind wandered off.

When the program ended, I joined the fellows, but Dave took me aside to share with me that he had given it considerable thought and prayer, and he was convinced the two of us should be together. It was my first of many experiences with the J. David Simonson who states what he wants to see happen and then refuses to take "no" for an answer. I was thrilled! Then I became concerned: I was dating a young man whose feelings I would hurt, but our date that night with Chris and Marlow convinced me that Dave was the one.

We had not been dating for too long when there was a big basketball tournament that I was looking forward to attending. I just had assumed Dave would ask me to go, but when it was almost the day of the tournament and I had heard nothing, I was hurt and decided that I would go anyway. There was another young man who had repeatedly asked me out, and he happened to ask again on that particular day. I am sure I surprised him when I said "yes." Actually, I surprised myself! Like Dave, he was very athletic; he was actually the coach for the local Golden Gloves boxing club.

When we arrived at the gymnasium the night of the tournament, the place was already full of people, and I was worried that we would not find a place to sit. My date assured me, though, that we would have ringside seats, because he had two of his Golden Glove boxers sparring for exhibition during half-time. To make conversation, I asked the names of the boxers. "Dave

Simonson and . . ." After hearing Dave's name, everything else became a blur. I suddenly wanted to go home because I had a feeling things were only going to go downhill from there.

I was right. When I sat down next to my date, Dave saw me and became very upset. I was very upset. My date did not have a clue what was going on, except that his boxers did an exceptional job and made him proud.

I did not hear from Dave at all for the next few days, and my heart was breaking. I called my dear friend, Ken, to seek counsel. Ken was like a brother to me, and I felt sure that Dave would have confided in him. Anyway, Ken was not in their room, and Dave answered the phone instead. How differently my life may have played out if Dave had hung up the phone rather than share his feelings! That enabled us to talk through that first difficult situation. Oh, yes, praise the Lord!

One weekend, on a visit home, my father asked, "Who is your boyfriend now?" I guess he sensed that this one was of greater interest than others. When I told him, "David Simonson," he asked if I knew who his father was. "Rev. Rudolph Simonson," I replied. He chuckled and told me that he and Rudy had been roommates at the seminary. I couldn't believe it—another connection.

My first meeting with Dave's parents was a disaster. His brother, Paul, was also attending Concordia and was dating Bonnie, a member of Rudolph's congregation who lived just down the block from them. The four of us had just attended an athletic banquet and then Paul had driven us all to Audubon to the Simonson's home. As Paul and David were saying goodnight to Bonnie and me in front of Bonnie's home, this flashlight was shined in my face by an irate woman who said, "Buddy Simonson! Are you going to stay up all night and neck?" Dave replied, "Mom, I'd like you to meet Eunice." There was no response from her, and this only added to my deep sense of hurt and embarrassment.

While I was staying at Bonnie's home, I was going to be eating meals with the Simonsons at the parsonage. Rudolf was very kind and tried hard to make me feel welcome, but it was very apparent that Mrs. Simonson did not really care for this new girlfriend Dave had brought into their home. Dave and I spent most of the weekend walking, as he tried to explain his mother's reaction to me. Only after many years of marriage did I truly feel she accepted me with love.

Neither Dave nor I had money, so most of our dating was at school events. He often sold his blood to have money to be able to include dinner on a night out. This made a deep impression on me—that he would go to such lengths to provide a lovely experience for us.

Dave and me going on a date

During his junior year and my sophomore year, we felt God's call. He decided to become a pastor, and I decided to go into nursing. We both knew that our lives would be spent together in whatever way God willed. Dave's proposal of marriage was beautifully worded, and my acceptance was a teary, "Yes!"

Fairview

When Dave felt God's call to go into the ministry, during his junior year at Concordia, our future plans changed as well. We knew we would face the future together in whatever way God led us. Dave continued the classes for his biology major but added those that would prepare him for the ministry. I decided to enter nurses' training. Again, I was making changes in mid-year, having completed two years at Concordia College. These had been such meaningful years, and it was painful to leave both the college and Dave.

I was accepted into the spring class of Fairview Hospital School of Nursing in January 1950. Concordia was connected to this school of nursing in Minneapolis, Minnesota, and my pre-med courses fit into the program nicely.

The hospital and the adjacent nurses' dorm were located near the Mississippi River, a lovely location with great facilities. Our comfortable dorm rooms were for two, and I was pleased to have a fine roommate, Chris (not my childhood friend, Chris).

We were a small class and a very interesting mix that added much to our life together. There were many common denominators, too. All were Christian girls with the motivation to become caregivers. A couple of the girls each said they hoped to meet and marry a doctor—they succeeded. Four of us had our futures planned with students at Luther Seminary in St. Paul, across the river.

We had great teachers. I remember one—Ms. McKain, who came from Texas and had a charming southern drawl. One quote we always remembered was on the transmission of germs: "It is said that a major transmission of germs is kissing, but I believe there is enough heat generated in a kiss to kill any living organism." Many years later she came to visit us in Tanzania.

When we came to some of the practical nursing care, I always seemed to volunteer as the "patient" in many procedures. The day we were taught how to give IM (intramuscular) injections, a buttock was needed, and mine was offered. The insertion of the big needle went easily but when my student withdrew the needle, I screamed! As the instructor looked at the needle, she told the class, "One should always check your needles before injection because some may have been damaged during the sharpening and have hooks." Thanks a lot!

The day we received our caps and gowns was thrilling. We all attended a service where we were dressed in our "whites" and the Fairview cap was placed on our heads. We were also given beautiful capes that were navy blue and lined with red. Did we ever feel important as we began doing patient care! Many stories came from the experiences that we shared each evening.

We had a choir, and rehearsal gave us a nice break from study. Our only "concert tour" was across the river at Luther Seminary. We marched in with heads held high, wearing our whites adorned with our newly-acquired caps and navy capes. We were so admired by our audience that several dates resulted after our performance.

Our psychiatric affiliation was completed at the state hospital in Fergus Falls, Minnesota. This experience was an eye-opener for all of us, as we met patients who were also regarded at times as "inmates." I had many mixed emotions about these misunderstood souls; some had been there for years, while others were newly admitted. Shock therapy was frightening and my first time to handle the tongue blade, when the shock was given, was for a giant of a man named Clancy. Clancy was known to be violent, so it was necessary for him to be shackled. I was terrified as I watched him led into the shock therapy room. The procedure went well, but I was thankful to complete that assignment.

We did have some fun moments during our time at the state hospital. I remember all of us nurses putting on a dance for the patients and dancing with those that were able. The orderlies were on alert in case their assistance was needed, because some of the patients were known to become aggressive. Little did I know at that time I would be very appreciative of those orderlies. One gentleman I danced with refused to let me go and I endured some tense moments before I received the help of an orderly who was able to come to my rescue.

I must admit the psych affiliation was not the favorite part of my training but it was certainly educational, worthwhile, and further helped me to realize that nursing was truly my calling. I was deeply touched by the lives of both teachers and patients— another of God's connections.

CHAPTER THREE

Love and Marriage

Weding, June 14, 1952

As soon as the change was made in the Nursing School's policy to allow students to marry while in training, Dave and I became officially engaged on October 12, 1951. I was to complete my studies several months earlier than my class, so the wedding day was set. Even the seminary had changed their policy allowing students to marry!

We set the earliest date possible. We were totally into this, with little or no regard as to how we would finance a wedding, where we would live and what we would live on. We just wanted to be married! Our parents were skeptical and asked us these questions, but they finally gave in and agreed to our getting married. Both Dave and I found five days in June that we could have time off—I from my class and work schedule and Dave from his summer construction job in Eau Claire, Wisconsin.

I designed and sewed my wedding gown plus the gowns of the five bridesmaids. Mine was white satin with a lace-covered bodice and long lace sleeves. The bridesmaids were in my favorite colors, yellow and green. My maid of honor was in frosted yellow organdie, with white daisies and the others were in dresses of the same fabric but in green. When and how I managed to complete these wedding arrangements is a mystery to me. I can only imagine there were many willing and helping hands.

There seemed to be no problem in the choice of attendants. My maid of honor was my "sister," Chris Rotto; and my lifelong Primrose friend, Delores Davidson; Kathryn Thorsgaard, my Oak Grove roommate; Lois Tomhave, my Fairview classmate; and Carol Villesvik, my cousin and "sister" were bridesmaids. Dave's attendants included his three brothers: Luther, Paul, and James, with Luther serving as his best man. Harold Nordby, my brother,

The wedding party

At the altar in Bang
Lutheran Church

and Robert Villesvik, my cousin and "brother" were also his attendants.

Invitations were sent, and the wonderful members of Father's congregations offered and provided the beautifully detailed reception. The Bang congregation had just completed building a beautiful brick church, and Dave and I were its inaugural wedding couple. Rosie Rud agreed to be our organist, brother Harold sang "The Lord's Prayer," and our fathers shared in performing the marriage service.

I arrived at my parents' home together with aunts, uncles, cousins, and friends on Friday, with Dave and his family arriving later that evening. The parsonage was so packed with people that our neighbors had to take the overflow.

Saturday morning arrived hot and sunny. I had hardly slept for days, but the excitement kept me flying. Taking Father's car, I drove from farm to farm to beg for peonies to decorate the church. The only flowers we could afford to buy were my bridal bouquet of yellow roses and white stephanotis and the little nosegays of white daisies for the bridesmaids. Mother was welcoming, cooking, and directing activities at the house, while two of my aunts were putting the final stitches to the hem of my gown.

With our parents: Edward & Olga Nordby (left) and Gladys and Rudolph Simonson (right)

Off we go!!

We had no wedding rehearsal and very few defined activities, yet by the early afternoon I was ready to bathe and dress. But, alas, all the rooms in our house were occupied. I again took Father's car to the next farm and asked if I could use their bathroom to get ready for my wedding. How everyone managed to get dressed and to the church in time remains a mystery, but we did!

When we arrived at the church, Dave and his attendants were dressed in the white jackets and black trousers they had rented. They looked so handsome!

The wedding and reception had been so beautiful, followed by a drive around the countryside in a friend's convertible. Accompanied by the love and laughter of our family and friends, it had all been so romantic.

The Honeymoon

Our dear friend, Jim Klobuchar, in his book, *The Cross Under the Acacia Tree*, relates the beginning of our "honeymoon" in a humorous way, but I can assure you that at the time, being stranded in Hillsboro, North Dakota, was far from humorous. But, as with all things, the passage of time has enabled us, too, to laugh at this story's retelling: We had three days before I needed to return to Fairview Hospital and Dave to Eau Claire, Wisconsin. After the beauty of our wedding and reception, things seemed to go a bit crazy. When Dave's dad rescinded the offer of the family car at the last minute, our dream of spending our first night in a hotel in Detroit Lakes, Minnesota, a community near his parents' home in Audubon, came to an immediate halt. Dave's brother, Paul, graciously offered to drive us to our honeymoon accommodations. Unfortunately, near Hillsboro, North Dakota, the car ran out of gas, and the owner of the only gas station in town was spending an overnight in (of all places) Detroit Lakes. Our wedding night was spent in the back seat of Paul's stranded car during a dreary rainstorm, while Paul and his girlfriend, Bonnie, were in the front seat. This was not the romantic setting we had envisioned for our first night as husband and wife. I didn't know whether to laugh or cry, so I did both.

The gas station opened at 6:00 a.m. and we were on our way. When we got to Detroit Lakes to check into our hotel, we were told that we would have to check out by 10:00 a.m.; that gave us only two hours—but enough of that story.

After leaving our hotel, we were collected and taken to Audubon, to celebrate the twenty-fifth wedding anniversary of Dave's parents, Rudolph and Gladys. Their church had planned a lovely reception following the church service. About all I remember of the occasion was that I sang a solo, "Oh, Perfect Love."

That evening, having no money and no place to sleep, my new mother-in-law, Gladys, sent me to Bonnie's house, a few blocks away from the parsonage, where three of us girls shared a bed, while Dave stayed at his parent's home. The one redeeming thought we clung to was that we would be alone together at my aunt Gladys' home in Minneapolis. She and her new husband, Charles, and her two teenage children, Bob and Carol, had been in our wedding and had offered their home for our last day together, as they were on vacation. We were given a key, and left Audubon in Paul's car. We were alone at last.

Dave and I enjoyed a wonderful day at my aunt's home, playing house and making plans for the weeks ahead when we would be apart. My heart ached at the thought of parting just as we were enjoying a new dimension of our love. In our eagerness to be married, we had done so little long-range planning, and now reality was beginning to sink in. The cautions we had been given were meant for our well-being. Well, we at least had our last evening together, alone—or so we thought. Just as Dave and I were about to retire to an upstairs bedroom, Gladys and her family walked through the front door, apologizing that they needed to return earlier than anticipated. I was offered a bed with cousin Carol, and Dave could sleep on the small sofa downstairs. When Carol fell asleep, I spent the remaining hours on the sofa with Dave.

So many details of this time have slipped from my memory but what remains is a sense of wonder and thankfulness that we can laugh at the situation we found ourselves in and appreciate the lessons we learned.

Hillside Attic

Before we parted, after our first few days of marriage, Dave told me of an offer he had received from a relative, Rev. Magnus Dahlen, that we could live in the attic of their two-story house on Hillside Avenue in St. Paul, located just a few blocks from the seminary. It was an uninsulated attic with two dormer windows, and if Dave would fix it up we could live with him and his family rent free. We now had a place to stay on the weekends, if we were given time off. We went to the local Goodwill store near the seminary, where we purchased a mattress and a few other essentials. We were allowed to share the bathroom on the second floor.

With the money Dave earned on his construction job, we were able to buy more needed things for our "castle in the air." By the time I had completed my schooling and Dave had re-turned to the seminary, we had moved into our borrowed attic permanently. With Dave's ideas and skills, we were able to make our first home cozy. Wooden crates from the grocery store became cupboards, an old table and chair set took on a new shine, we were able to get our mattress into a frame, and I had a sink with water. It was grand!

I was now a registered nurse, and I needed to find a job. I found a good position as a surgical nurse at Miller Hospital in downtown St. Paul, with hours that perfectly matched the hours needed for Dave's studies; 7:00 a.m. to 3:00 p.m. We would awaken early, and I would catch the streetcar on Como Avenue to downtown and Dave would walk to the seminary. I enjoyed my new job and the staff at Miller Hospital very much, as well as the drama of the surgery itself. I was able to scrub with surgeons who were fast becoming famous, such as Dr. Foley and Dr. Wagenstien.

The autumn months passed quickly, and then the Minnesota winter set in. Our cozy little attic apartment became a fridge overnight. Dave soon had our little home perfect again by installing insulation and purchasing a space heater.

By mid-November, we had the joy of knowing we were expecting our first child. Fortunately I felt great, and I also had peace of mind knowing my obstetrician was the one I most admired at Fairview. Dr. Bacon assured me that I was "just made for having babies," which were words I cherished.

As spring approached, Dave was given a job at the seminary as an assistant domestic environmental engineer—or janitor as they were called in those days. He would have this position until graduation.

Luther Place

With the acceptance of the job at the seminar came a three-room apartment just across the street from the school. We thanked our gracious host and hostess for their gift of our first little attic home and moved into this partially furnished apartment (kitchen cupboards, table, and chair) with the few things we had acquired. This was perfect for a heavily pregnant lady like me, as all was at ground level.

I continued to work in surgery at Miler Hospital in downtown St. Paul until two weeks before my due date. The last month, I was moved to eye surgery where I was able to sit a bit more. My time at Miller Hospital gave me experiences and learning skills which became very useful in the years ahead in Africa.

Stephen Daniel was born on August 1, 1953, a healthy, energetic baby from his first breath. What joy he brought! I was very happy to have three months just caring for him and his proud dad before it was necessary for me to resume work.

This time I went to work at Fairview Hospital in Minneapolis, where I was put on a medical-surgical floor. This was the kind of nursing I really enjoyed, as I cared for those who were not sedated like those in surgery. Being back with some of my classmates and instructors was good. Since I wanted to take care of Steve during much of the day, I asked to be on what was called the relief shift (3:00 p.m. to 11:00 p.m.). We had a lovely girl take care of Steve from two until Dave came home at four. I was home at midnight to nurse Steve and catch a little sleep.

Steve provided many amazing experiences during that first year. He walked by ten months, ran by eleven months, climbed anything climbable at one year. One episode, when he was eleven months old, could have been fatal for him, and I could have been charged with child neglect. I had settled him down for a nap and was using this free time to get some neglected projects done. There was a call from the open kitchen door (it was a hot July day) and, leaving my work, I ran to find a police man holding Steve.

"Is this your child, ma'am?"

Steve was wearing only his baggy diapers, holding a hammer in one hand and Dave's pipe in the other, looking a bit scared and hot. Somehow, he had escaped me, collected these goodies, and wandered into the very busy intersection on Como Avenue, stopping traffic and bringing the police. "Does anyone know who this baby belongs to?"

Fortunately, one of our seminary friends recognized Steve and told the policeman where we lived. The shame and thankfulness I felt still moves me. This was but one episode with this adventurous baby. As I realized I was pregnant again, I could only pray for strength and wisdom.

I continued to work at Fairview Hospital, but only into the fifth month of pregnancy. It was not considered suitable for pregnant women to be working on the floor. It was a good decision to remain at home with Steve.

At this time, another important direction was given to us. Again God used the man, who had given me the prophecy that I would someday go to his Maasai: Dr. Richard Reusch. He was now retired from his mission work and was teaching at Gustavus Adolphus College in St. Peter, Minnesota. He came to give lectures at the seminary to challenge the seminarians to consider foreign missions. He met and spoke to Dave and announced, "You are the man for my Maasai!" I will always remember that day, when Dave came home that evening and asked, "Would you be willing to go to Africa?"

We made that decision together, with great jubilation and prayer. Only then did I tell Dave about my meeting with Dr. Reusch, when I was fifteen years old.

This decision and the church's encouragement gave Dave the desire to work on a master's degree in missions. Upon completing the third year at seminary, Dave focused on the Maasai tribe, researched and met those who had worked with and had written about them. This degree would be the first given in missionology from Luther Seminary, in connection with the University of Minnesota.

We were very fortunate to be allowed to live in our Luther Place apartment. When my due date drew near, I asked Dr. Bacon if he would allow Dave to be with me during delivery. Up to this time no one was allowed this privilege, but I continued to plead, "We are going to Africa and it might be necessary for Dave to deliver other babies." He laughingly agreed and gave Dave instructions on how he would have to pose as a doctor so no one else would ask for this favor.

On the big evening when I was admitted, Dave dressed in gown and cap with the doctor. As I was being wheeled into one delivery room, another woman was on her way into another. We wished each other good luck. We both delivered within a few minutes of each other and then were put into a double room.

Naomi Ruth was the beautiful baby born on November 23, 1954. Dave had been allowed a part in helping bring her into this world and supporting me all the way through.

Dave came into the room, still dressed in his doctor's garb and rushed to me with great emotion and joy. "You were wonderful" he said, kissing and hugging me with passion. When Dave left the room, my roommate exclaimed, "Where did you ever find a doctor like that?"

Now we had two little ones, and life was rich and full. Our parents were delighted with the grandchildren and tried to come as often as they could. My parents lived in western North Dakota at this time, so they found it difficult to come often. As we shared with them the possibility of going to Africa, I expected they might show disappointment, as we would be taking their only grandchildren. However, they were delighted and told us of the great wish they had held to go as missionaries to China. My father's health prevented their going, so they emphasized mission work in all their congregations. I grew up with this strong

With Naomi and Steve

interest, inspired by all the visiting missionaries my parents invited to our home and churches.We would fulfill that mission dream.

When the call came from the American Lutheran Church to go to Tanganyika, our focus centered on preparations. Dave completed his masters degree and was ordained at Central Lutheran Church in Minneapolis, along with several other men who had answered the mission call. We would be going for five years. What things would we need? We were given many ideas and suggestions from the church/mission office and from missionaries on leave. Barrels were bought and much time spent at Goodwill finding household needs, medical supplies, and clothes (incuding clothes for our children—another was expected in the next year. It was an exciting and exhausting time. We were encouraged by so many people, and offers of help came often. Our dear friends, Bill and Lynn Smith, had also been called to Tanganyika. At meetings of seminary wives, Lynn and I would share our dreams, apprehensions, and excitement. They left for Tanganyika a year ahead of us. Our lives were connected in many ways in the years ahead.

As the time drew near for our departure, the mission board decided they wanted Dave to fill a position of pastor/teacher at the mission's Teacher Training Center at Marangu on Mt. Kilimanjaro. This change in appointment required another change: Dave would need to "anglicize" his existing American teaching certificate to comply with the British educational system. To do this, we had to go to England first, where Dave attended the University of London; the children and I would live at Hothorp Hall. It was another of God's amazing "connections" for us.

CHAPTER FOUR

To Africa and the First Year

England

With all the change of plans, the mission board decided to send us by ship from New York on The Queen Elizabeth! And we were placed in cabin class rather than steerage!

The farewells were not easy. Our parents and other family members were at the St. Paul depot to put us on the train to New York. This was an adventure in itself. With our eight-month-old Naomi and one-and-a-half-year-old Steve, plus many bags and boxes, we were an amazing sight, I am sure. Dave had been advised to bring his sixteen-bore shotgun, .357 caliber Ruger pistol, and ammunition with him. This created a number of "challenges" along the journey, as they needed to be checked in with all the police everywhere we went.

New York was overwhelming in its size and frantic activity; I still wonder how we made it to the hotel where we stayed two days. Dave needed to check in with the Lutheran World Federation offices; the kids and I were told not to go out.

Boarding the Queen Elizabeth was yet another adventure. I held Naomi and tried to keep Steve in hand while Dave went through the gun regime. The six-day crossing was made exciting by so many new experiences.

The Queen Elizabeth

There was a nursery for little ones, which gave me time to settle in. One day Steve managed to escape the nursery and, after a frantic search, was found on the ships forward keel. We were sternly advised to keep him with us at all times.

The ship docked first at Cherborough, France, and we were allowed to get off to explore for a few hours. I was deeply touched by the ravages of war in that once-lovely city. We met people we knew as we walked the narrow streets; they were also on the way to mission fields, but alas, they were in steerage.

The next docking was in North Hampton, England. The gun drama continued as Dave had to leave me once again with our other stuff and our little ones. Again Steve escaped, and another frantic search ensued. Abandoning our luggage, I ran out to the docks where Steve, with little feet at the very edge of the dock, was looking down the forty-foot drop to the ocean below. I sat Naomi down and ran, praying fervently he would not be distracted and fall in. I grabbed him and began to cry. For months I had nightmares about this!

Guns cleared, baggage checked on a train, kids subdued, and parents barely speaking to each other, we were on our way to London! The sights I remember most clearly were the houses closely set together and each with at least two chimneys; I had never seen so many. It seemed the cities could have been painted in various shades of grey. In London, we transferred to another train which took us to Market Harborough in the midlands of England. I felt like we were stepping into the world of Bronte. The villages, with quaint buildings and lovely gardens, were beautiful.

Lloyd Swantz had studied at Luther Seminary, a year or two ahead of Dave. He had been sent to England with the purpose of

helping Lutherans from the countries suffering from the war. He had learned of an estate that was being considered for demolition. It had an interesting history, the last owner having been Field Marshall Montgomery. It had been used to house children from areas of London that were in danger of getting bombed. The huge house was

Hothorp Hall, England

surrounded by neglected gardens, abandoned tile-covered stables, and exuded an aura of history. I found it all mysterious and intriguing. Lloyd was able to buy this hall, and he had gathered an amazing group of refugees to live there.

We were given a room on the second floor. It was huge, with high ceilings and what was meant to be a fireplace/heater which didn't work. The room was sparsely furnished, with four single beds and a baby cot, a clothes cupboard, and a couple of chairs. I think we shared a bathroom with other guests. The biggest challenge was the long stairway, which I seemed to spend too much time climbing up and down after Steve. This activity was impeded by my now very pregnant body.

Dave settled us into our space and headed back to London. He shared an apartment with two Tanganyikans who were to become yet another amazing connection.

The Hothorp "family" was an unusual mix of people, and I never heard how they all came to be at Hothrop. Lloyd made each one of us feel welcome. There was an Estonian family with two young children—how I wish I could remember their names. The children were very fond of Steve, and that was great. Language was a challenge, but love and kindness gave us the communication we needed most of the time. I would have liked to have known their story.

John—the only name I remember of this Polish refugee—was the designated cook. Food supplies were short, but the American Relief program had given Lloyd a great supply of cheese—good cheddar. John seemed to find a way of putting cheese into everything. I made a little ditty about this:

John's cheese cake and cheese potato pie,

If you don't like cheese,

At least you better try.

A group of three women from Finland who were preparing to go to Tanganyika were learning English and Swahili. We shared so much in common, and I enjoyed their dedication. Lloyd had married Marja, a classmate at Luther Seminary, from Finland. She was already working as a teacher in Ashira Girls School on Mt. Kilimanjaro. She did come for a time (perhaps at Christmas?) and we all were so thrilled and happy for Lloyd. At our first posting at Marangu, we were near Ashira so these "connections" were lasting.

A refugee from Hungary named Julius was also at Hothorp. He had been in some amazing escape and brought many skills in renovating the hall and stables. Dave often came weekends and enjoyed working with Julius. He became a dear friend also. We reconnected with him thirty years later, when he had moved to Canada and googled Dave's name, finding us on one of our furloughs.

Many people visited Hothorp and brought new interests. One group came from an American air base. Some of these men had families in the States and were missing their children. Naomi was an adorable baby, who loved being passed around by these "daddies." Church leaders and others interested in missionary activity often visited.

Being that I was in my third trimester of pregnancy, I was told I needed to be registered with the National Health Service. A doctor would come to examine me and then "reservations" could be made at the hospital in Market Harborough. This doctor arrived in a small sports car, and I invited him up to our room. Being used to exams, I modestly lay down and exposed my tummy. This seemed to shock the doctor, who quickly covered me and felt my extended abdomen and exclaimed, "Yes, yes, indeed you are pregnant." So nice to have this confirmed.

So many thoughts went through my mind: "I hope he won't be the one to deliver the baby," "I'm embarrassed," and more. He asked my due date, and I said January 26. After writing this in his book, he advised me to attend clinic and follow all instructions of the midwife, who would be doing the delivery. With relief, I promised to do that and went in the next day.

The Midlands has been the area of "the hunt," I was told, and one lovely autumn day a group of people on horseback appeared with their hounds. Again, I had the feeling of being in a story as they rode off at the sound of a bugle, with the hounds yipping excitedly. Hothorp had been a starting point for the chase, I was told, but I never learned if the fox was near or if there even was one.

I was invited one evening to dine with a group of church folk in Theddingworth. Our "family" at Hothorp Hall offered to care for Steve and Naomi. It was a delightful dinner, although I realized how proper these people could be and felt a bit gauche. The one memory of the evening came as I was answering questions from the gentlemen on either side of me. They asked about our mission call, our education, and many other things. I had mentioned I was a nurse and hoped to use that training in Africa. Then one gentleman asked if I had ever been in the theater. I was flattered to think he recognized some acting ability and answered modestly, "Only a few productions." The look on his face told me right away that I had goofed; theater meant operating room. We managed to set this straight and had a good laugh. There is English, and then there is English!

As the winter began, a new routine was established. Besides wearing warmer clothes, we were given water bottles, which we would bring to the big kitchen to have filled with hot water. We then placed them in our beds; the sheets always felt a bit damp. Hothorp had "central heating"—a big furnace in the "center" of the basement never functioned. Even though I had grown up in below-zero temperatures in North Dakota, I had never felt the cold so acutely. We were given small heaters, but one needed to use them carefully as the expense was high.

Christmas was a special time, and everyone bought something from their traditions to the celebration. A tree was set up in the ballroom, and we created the decorations. Dave had some days to be with us, which was the best part.

I had been faithful with my appointments with the hospital in Market Harborough and my expectations were mixed. I was much bigger than I had been with the other two, so wondered how delivery would be. The matron was like someone out of a comic strip—big, dour, with a big buckle on her belt. I tried very hard to win her friendship, but I guess that just "isn't done." She had a chip on her shoulder about Americans. When she heard I was a nurse, she really froze. She reminded me that I was registered to deliver on January 26 Did all English women deliver as registered? Dave came to be with me the days before, and on January 26 labor began. He took me in and expected to remain with me in the labor room.

"You Americans have such strange expectations." At the look on my face the matron said, "It is still visiting hours so you can stay until they are over". We had noted another couple coming in at this time, the husband giving his wife a kiss in the cheek wishing her "Good luck" and "Cheerio."

The labor progressed quickly and just as visiting hours ended, Dave and I prayed together and he left. I was taken into the delivery room; the matron was to deliver me! I foolishly asked, "Will I need an episiotomy? I had that with the first two." She scoffed, grabbed my legs, and said, "Get on with it!" I did just that and tore seriously. Nathan was a beautiful, healthy, big nine-pound boy. Nathan David Simonson, born January 26, 1956. The next hour was torture. "Oh dear," the matron said, "we need to call the doctor to do the repair."

A half hour later, the doctor—he of the shiny sports car—arrived. My fears mounted. He became very professional, and I relaxed until the matron informed him there were no anesthetics available. "She will need something," the doctor replied. A tank of some sort was wheeled in but was nearly empty. I leave the rest of this drama to the imagination of the reader.

Safely settled in a six-bed ward, the next day I began to recover and was delighted with our new son. Dave was pleased with Nathan; he had to leave for London after viewing his strong son.

"Ten days of required bed rest" was the rule of matron and hospital. Secretly I would exercise and even walk about when no one was looking—we American nurses tend to self treat. I enjoyed my roommates who found it fun to share their impressions of Americans: You speak English in such nasal tones, they told me. I replied and mimicked the several ways they said the word "love": luv, loov, loovee.

When Julius, the Hungarian from Hothorp, came with flowers and great expressions of admiration, my roommates were amazed at my "husband"—a bit of déjà-vu from birthing Steve. I was well cared for and thankful.

Returning to Hothorp and the support of everyone made the days ahead a lot easier to handle. The "family" had cared for Steve and Naomi very well, and they were delighted with baby Nathan. Dave came for weekends until his courses were finished and then was with us as we prepared to leave for Tanganyika.

Dear friends from seminary days, Bill and Lynn Smith, were returning to Tanganyika after being in the States. They had been serving in Tanganyika for a year when he contracted polio and was evacuated with his family of wife and three little ones back to the States for treatment. The brave outlook he and Lynn shared gave us encouragement. They spent a few days with us at Hothorp, during which time we had the baptism of Nathan David; they became his godparents.

Three weeks after Nathan's birth, we were on our way!

Hunting Clan

Dave wanted to save the mission board some money, so he checked around to find the least-expensive line going to East Africa, and came up with the Hunting Clan. The name itself gave me pause; we were not going hunting, but we did have the guns and ammo. A retired, non-pressurized DC3 that still bore some war scars was to be our transport to Nairobi, Kenya.

How we got to Heathrow Airport is gone from my memory, but the flight had enough excitement to remember. Since the plane could only do the flight in daylight and at a low altitude, the journey took three days.

The Hunting Clan's DC3

We landed in Nice, France, on day one to re-fuel, then flew on to Malta where we were put up in a lovely hotel. Dave helped me settle our three little ones; we decided to eat in shifts so as not to leave them alone. Dave went first, as I was still nursing Nathan. When all three were asleep, I went to the dining room to join Dave, but he was at a table with pilot and crew, so I sat alone. I sent a message, via the waiter, to Dave telling him he could join me. The waiter returned and replied, looking rather puzzled, "The gentleman says he will see you in the morning." Dave meant it as a joke (ha ha!) and later joined me back at the room.

On day two we needed to be up pre-dawn to be at the airport for a dawn takeoff. Bundling up our little ones once more, we were off to Juba, Wadi Halfa, and Khartoum. We had some very bumpy weather; Dave and Naomi were airsick. As there were no stewardesses to help, I was kept very busy.

Our first glimpse of Africa was so exciting. As we landed in Juba, we saw camels crossing the desert, which delighted us all. Landing just at sunset in Khartoum was another picture memory (we had no camera) straight out of *National Geographic*— mosques, Arabs in robes, and women in their *Gad rah*. This time our hotel accommodations were a bit shabby, and we were fed with the children. As I gave Naomi her glass bottle before sleep, she threw it out of her cot and broke it. She set up a great howl, so I spent most of the night nursing her with Nathan.

After an almost sleepless night, day three began, and we were once again on our way. As we waited to board the plane, Steve managed to escape. This time, he went to the flat roof of the airport where several Arabs were sleeping with their heads covered by cloth. We found him happily pulling these cloths off and cheerily saying, "Good morning!" Have Arab and American relations improved?

The only stop I remember on this flight to Nairobi was Kampala. The African scenery had changed dramatically from desert to lush greenery and from camels to busy traffic of cars, trucks, and buses.

As we finally reached Nairobi and disembarked, we felt we were a part of an interesting group. Many passengers left in Kampala, others were returning Kenyans, some were actually going hunting, and a few were first timers like us. Dave had enjoyed his time with the crew. We wished each other goodbye as new found friends.

Nairobi

Stan Benson, my cousin, had been working in Tanganyika for over a year as an agriculturalist and missionary. We had been in correspondence with him through the year and he had offered to meet us in Nairobi, Kenya, and bring us to Tanganyika. We were looking forward to this and the time we would share.

It is important to note that during this period in Kenya, 1952-1960, the Mau Mau Rebellion was going on. This was an insurgency, a militant African National movement, with the aim of removing British and European settlers. Many Africans were also killed by the Mau Mau, for refusing to take the Mau Mau oath to kill white people. It was a very violent, bloody time.

Alas, when we finally arrived, February 1956, at the airport, there was no sign of Stan or anyone who seemed to be connected or interested in us. The airport was a simple wooden structure on raised footings. Dave gathered all our belongings in a pile, with the kids and me sitting on a bench nearby. The guns and ammo boxes were given to me to sit on with the words, "Remember these are dangerous times with the Mau Mau everywhere. There is a death penalty on losing guns." And with that, Dave left us to search for some person who could help. Clutching Nathan and sitting on the ammo made it impossible for me to control Steve, who again went exploring, and Naomi, who was stuck under a bench across the room. Welcome to Nairobi!

Thankfully, Dave found a phone book and phone. In looking for church-related guest homes, he found the one run by the African Inland Church. Connections! Stan was staying there and had booked space for us. A fine couple who ran this guest house told us that Stan had been told by the Hunting Clan office that our plane would be 24 hours late, so he had gone to a movie. These gracious people said they would come as quickly as possible to get us. An hour later, we were packed into the car and headed into Nairobi. What a glorious feeling to be this far and received so warmly! The only note of displeasure came when they learned we had these guns. There was a deep sense of fear for everyone those days because of the Mau Mau. A secure place was found for the guns, and we were assured of God's care. When Stan returned that evening, he felt so sorry that he had not been at the airport to greet us. But we were together, and the next day we would be on our way to Tanganyika. He told us that Bill and Lynn Smith and family had arrived the day before on British Overseas Airlines and had been met by Bob Johnson, another Luther Seminary classmate also serving in Tanganyika. We would all be reunited at a mission gathering a few days after arriving in Tanganyika. The excitement grew as we neared our destination.

After a good night's sleep, we were ready to pack up again. By this time we were truly a motley crew, with one bag stuffed with dirty diapers and soiled clothes. The kids were holding up well, and we were on our way. So many new and exciting things to see: the women were walking with heavy loads on their heads; vegetation different than we had ever seen before; and as we moved out of the city into flat savanna, we saw our first wild animals. Gazelle, zebra, wildebeest, and giraffe were roaming free, and the sight thrilled me so much.

We had been traveling on the dusty road for several hours when Stan stopped. In the ditch was an abandoned car with the front screen smashed. "That is Bob Johnson's car," Stan told us. He and Dave checked it out and saw no sign of violence or injury. They could not understand what had happened. My first dramatic thought was that the Mau Mau had taken all the family hostage—or worse. There were no clues, no luggage or papers but Stan knew the car. Stan said we should just carry on.

We had gone only a few miles when our car stopped. The men checked it and found that a stone or rock had smashed the gas tank and all the fuel was gone. Stan found an empty fuel can, told us he would walk to the next town, Namanga, which was only "a few miles" away. He hoped to be picked up if any cars came along, so we should just be comfortable until he returned. Comfortable??? We had just seen Johnson's abandoned car, Mau Mau lurked behind every bush, and we were to be sitting hostages. Being in this uncomfortable situation worked serious damage to my peace of mind.

Nothing happened. After an hour, Stan was dropped off by a passing car with enough gas to get us to Namanga. How about the hole in the gas tank? "No problem." I would soon learn that this statement was the preface to imaginative solutions. Stan found a bar of soap, cut a big piece, and wedged it into the hole. After filling the tank with enough gas to reach Namanga, we were on our way. Namanga is where we would check into Tanganyika, and it was also a lovely spot to have a break, use the toilets, and enjoy briefly the beautiful garden of a hotel. Stan and Dave repaired the car, and we were on our way. A police post at the Tanganyika border cleared us. We were in the land to which God had called us!

Later we asked Bill Smith to recall the events of their arrival in Kenya:

As I recall, after receiving treatment for polio at Sister Kenny Institute in Minneapolis, we flew to Nairobi. Bob Johnson met us—Lynn, me, three-year old Scott, two-year old Brent, and infant Gregory—at the airport. I'm not sure, but I believe we began our trip to Arusha in a Peugeot. At any rate, it seems that somewhere along the way our windscreen (windshield) was shattered by a rock. We continued until all went *kaput* [broke down, went to pieces]. It may have been the transmission. At any rate the car was dead. We pushed it off the road somewhere between Nairobi and Namanga.

Fortunately, a large lorry loaded to the hilt (may have been gunias of maize or steel drums) was kind enough to offer help. The Indian driver agreed that Lyn and the baby could sit with him in the cab. Bob and I,, with the two small children, managed to squeeze ourselves into a three-foot empty space between the capacity load of the lorry and the tail gate. We were so very grateful to God for sending unexpected help in our dire need.

So it was, Lynn and baby bounced along safely up front, while Bob, the kids and I "ate dust" and tried to hang on at the rear. We were on our way home. How many times we have been surprised by God's grace, when he would send unexpected answers to our dilemmas.

Shigatini

We were reunited with Bill and Lynn, Bob and Esther Johnson, and introduced to the other missionaries—a joy with lasting connections.

Stan was still our driver for the next lap of our journey to the mission station of Shigatini, in the Pare Mountains. We would

The Pare Mountains

be living near Kerm and Dotty Youngdale for the next few months, to learn Swahili. With love and prayers from our new "family," we were on our way again.

Mt. Meru was so beautiful, and a sense of destiny touched me as we left. Banana trees, coffee trees, flowering trees—my love for trees has always been a strong connection to God's creation, and all these new varieties thrilled me. As we moved across the plains, Mt. Kilimanjaro came into view, majestic and spectacular. My entire being was in awe. Herds of zebra, some ostrich, and other new creatures delighted Steve and Naomi. Baby Nathan was content to sleep and nurse.

There seemed to be a constant movement of people as we drew near the city of Moshi, at the base of Mt. Kilimanjaro. It was a beautiful town with tree-lined streets. As we drove through the streets, Stan pointed out the area where the Lutheran church was involved.

The Pare Mountains are a long range of high cliffs with no special peaks. At a small village, Stan turned from the main road that continued to the coast and Dar es Salaam. We began a climb on a twisting, narrow road that wove its way to Shigatini. I hardly dared to look to the side of this rise; the view was great but there was little to prevent our dropping over the edge. What would happen if we were to meet a car or truck coming down? Stan would point out spots where vehicles had gone over the edge. Thanks a lot!

Thanking the Lord and heaving a sigh of relief, we arrived at a beautiful mission station where we were warmly welcomed by the Youngdales. They had three little boys who welcomed Steve enthusiastically. This began a warm and lasting friendship.

We were given a delicious lunch and taken to the guest house, where we would live. It had one large room with beds and cots as well as cupboards. We would share an outhouse and bathroom facilities with the Youngdales. We would use kerosene lanterns for lights. The Youngdales were so hospitable, providing our meals and meeting our needs. With good African staff, there were loving *ayahs* (nannies) for our children, so we would be able to study and attend the daily Swahili class taught to us by a fine primary school teacher, Eliakunda.

Eliakunda would come, after teaching at the mission primary school, and teach us for several hours. Swahili is a very phonetic language, so once the a-e-i-o-u sounds were memorized, we could read (although at first we did not understand). We could change a verb around by adding prefixes and suffixes; it was fun. I have always loved word games like Scrabble. One day, we studied "locatives"—here, there, and right here. These are delineated by very simple suffixes of *ko, po,* and *mo.* I struggled with this and Dave became very annoyed with me, wondering how I could be so stupid. That was it!! I stood up with tears streaming down my face, and said, "You can have your *ko, po, mo* and GO! I'm out of here!" Fortunately, the teacher remained and I came back, a little shame-faced.

The missionary meat supply was often replenished by the men going hunting—one of the things Dave had looked forward to. Three men came with their wives, who stayed with Dotty and me. While the men were off hunting, the supper conversation turned to storytelling—a sort of "can you top this" story. The women had been here for some time and had amazing stories, but when they started telling snake stories, I began to feel sick. The only fear I had of coming to Africa was that I might encounter snakes—a childhood fear from naughty boys chasing me with them. They told of a mother putting her child to bed, having a premonition that all was not right with the blanket, then lifting it to discover a coiled cobra.

That was enough for me. I gathered my three and took them up the hill to our house by lantern light. Then, as I held the baby, I had the other two stand in the middle of the room while I lifted the blankets. Assured that all was okay, I tucked them in and prayed with them. Just before I was ready for bed, while holding the lantern to blow it out, there was a rustling in the grass roof. Several black heads peeped out from the top of the wall, and I froze. "Snakes really like grass roofs," one of the women had said. My imagination went wild. I fell on my knees by the bed and began pleading with God to spare my children. I had some unkind things to say about Dave going off and leaving me to face the snakes on my own. God spoke to me, "My child, I did not call you here to be afraid. I am with you always." Amazing, yet very true. Thanking God, I slept in his peace. I learned the next day that these black creatures were skinks—a harmless type of lizard.

Marangu

It was hard to leave Shigatini; Dotty and Kerm had been so good to us. There were great moments with them, our teacher, and the Pare people. Dave had enjoyed being a part of the church building project, which provided the first of countless stories about his strength. He was with a group gathering rocks for buildings. One rock was too heavy for the men, but Dave lifted it himself and loaded it into a truck. The story grew with each telling. These introductions to people and language provided a good introduction to Tanganyika. Now we were ready for our first assignment at Marangu Teachers Training College.

The school was located on the lower slopes of Mt. Kilimanjaro, a beautiful spot with lush surroundings. All the buildings were on different levels of the slope; the house we were given was just above the main school building.

The snow covered dome of Mt Kilimanjaro, 19,340 ft, rising above the clouds

The house was built by the Germans who had started the school. What a wonderful place to live! A long stairway led to a veranda, where we entered into a spacious living/dining room. There were rooms for every one, and a bathroom of our own. Yeah!

The barrels we had packed for Africa somehow had arrived, filled with household goods and clothing for growing children. It was such fun unpacking and sorting—our own place at last!

We were welcomed by the staff of the school. First to greet us were the headmaster and his wife, the Overaas from Norway. The Gottneids, the Palms, and several Tanganyikans came with food and invitations to have meals with them until we got our supplies. We felt loved.

Dave began his work as pastor, teacher, and coach almost immediately. My time seemed to be fully occupied in child care. Steve and Naomi found much to explore and other missionary kids to play with. Naomi loved to take off her clothes and run down to the school, only to have embarrassed stu-dents bring her back again—our little wild child.

On the steps of our Marangu house with Steve, Naomi, and Nathan 1957

One event that I remember well happened several months after arriving in Marangu. Dave was playing with the children and had Steve on his shoulders. The ever-active Steve tried to stand on dad's shoulders, and he crashed down, head first, on the cement floor. He was concussed, and I watched in alarm as the pupil of his right eye dilated—a subdural hematoma, I figured. I knew he should be seen by a doctor. We asked Al and Alice Gottneid what and who we should see, and they urged us to take him to Nairobi. We had no car. They said they would take Steve and me. This was a truly amazing offer, because it would be a ten-hour trip. Dave would care for the other two, with the help of Martha, our wonderful *ayah* for the kids. I would give up nursing Nathan, as I would not be able to care for him after this crisis. After making quick arrangements, we were on our way. Early the next morning Steve was alert, but he said his head hurt and there was still no reaction in the right eye pupil.

The journey seemed endless and held none of the excite-ment we had felt as we traveled this dusty gravel road the first time. There was no concern for Mau Mau, only prayers that

Steve would be okay. We stopped for lunch at Namanga and then reached Nairobi in the late afternoon. We went to the Gertrude's Garden Children's Hospital where Steve was admitted and examined. They felt the hematoma would not increase and Steve would be fine, but they wanted to keep him for observation. I was told to return in the morning. It was so hard to leave my three year old, but he was in good hands—and God's hands.

Gottneids took me to the same guest house where we had been so lovingly cared for on our arrival, and the couple welcomed us warmly. I was in the first trimester of pregnancy and during the night I began to bleed. I was taken to the Kenyatta Hospital, where I lost the pregnancy and had a D + C. I was in one hospital and Steve in another; it was a time of testing for both of us. I was discharged after two days as was Steve, so we began the long trip home. My heart was heavy over the miscarriage and I missed Dave being with us. How would he feel about our loss? Rather than focus on this, my prayers of thanks for Steve became my focus.

It was wonderful to be back home with Dave and the kids. Life soon returned to normal, with each of us in our various roles and schedules.

Dave was a great coach and enjoyed preparing the men and boys for an upcoming track event to be held in Moshi. They would compete against several government schools and the Police Training Center—all very British. Having been a track and field athlete at Concordia, he was an excellent coach.

During this time he saw many Brits of his age participating. He asked if these events were open for everyone. The remembered response has become part of legend: "Take off your pants, padre, and show us what you can do." He broke the Tanganyika record in both discuss and shot-put. He then went on to coach the entire Tanganyika track team in both Uganda and Kenya competitions.

Rugby was a sport greatly enjoyed by the British. When some of the team watched him in the track events, they saw potential for their rugby team. He was invited to join the Moshi Club. This was the beginning of many years in rugby.

One of my favorite stories came from watching my first game. The Moshi Club had a set of bleachers, and I was sitting alone, in front of three wives of the other team members. They were having a rather catty talk about the "American chap" who had joined the team: "He was an American football player; they use all sorts of padding," My interest grew as they laughingly said he was wearing all that padding now. There was a "line out," right in front of us. The woman exclaimed, "My goodness! It's all him!" I muttered under my breath, "You better believe it, and he's *all* mine."

When Dave started playing rugby, there were those who felt it was not appropriate for a missionary, and perhaps it would take Dave away from his calling. He assured them that he would never miss a Sunday or mission meeting. In the twenty years he played, he kept that promise and he made many positive friendships and links in God's team. One time, he drove all the way back to Arusha after a game against the team in Mombasa, Kenya, on bumpy dirt roads with three broken ribs, just to be in the pulpit the next morning.

After a rugby game – Nathan, me, Dave, and Steve

Our mission family was wonderful—very caring and helpful. Dave felt a strong bond with his students, and several of them went on into the ministry while others became teachers. He felt God had a purpose for his time at Marangu, but there was still a strong pull towards the Maasai. Near the end of our first year at Marangu, one of the missionaries who was working among the Maasai decided to climb Kilimanjaro. This majestic mountain challenged many. Don Johnson climbed with the usual porters, and we wished him well. Before reaching the summit, he developed pulmonary edema and needed to be carried down. He was in serious condition but lived. It was felt he should not return to Nabarera in South Maasailand until he fully recovered. Would Dave be willing to take over the work there? The door opened, and another teacher was found to take Dave's classes. He was going to the Maasai! He was able (how, I do not know) to buy a three-ton truck and was off to Nabarera. The kids and I would remain in Marangu for several months.

Dave's first visit to Nabarera has become yet another legend. Jim Klobuchar recorded this in a way I never could duplicate in the book, *The Cross Under the Acacia Tree*. I just remember Dave coming home to Marangu totally exhausted. As he got into bed he said, "I killed a lion," and promptly fell asleep. I only learned the full story in the morning as he shared it at our devotions.

At his first meeting with the Maasai warriors they asked his help in killing a "man-eater" lion that had been terrorizing the village. They could kill the lion with their spears and become true members of the warriors' group, but they felt the support of a gun would be best. As Dave related the story to me, I could feel the emotional impact this experience had for him. He knew he couldn't refuse; he would be considered a coward. He agreed to their request, but only if he went alone. He felt both fear and excitement as he drove out to the wells, which he had been told were dug hundreds of years before by Phoenicians, and there he encountered the lion. He took his shotgun, got out of the truck, and by the light of the headlights he shot the lion as it sprang at him. As Dave shared this story with us, he shivered again with the remembrance. He said that when the lion lay dead at his feet, he fell to his knees sobbing and praying. When the warriors heard the shots, they came running. Dave rose to his feet and received their praise and acceptance, as a warrior of the Lord.

Dave needed to report the killing to the district officer, who thanked him and permitted him to keep the skin. The female lion measured ten feet, four inches, from tail to nose. The lion skin became one of our rugs. We have photos of our children, as they lay on this lion their daddy had killed. They loved hearing the story. We will always thank God for this lion which was used in God's plan as the perfect opening for Dave's work among the Maasai. My heart was filled with awe, amazement, and deep thankfulness that he was not hurt or killed.

Work in Maasailand kept Dave very busy. He needed to complete a classroom in one week, for government approval, so he worked all day and traveled to Arusha at night for supplies. We only saw him when that was completed. The extra seventy miles to Marangu from Arusha were just too much. One night

Dave was driving the lorry back to Marangu when he fell asleep at the wheel. The next thing he knew, he and the lorry were settled on the far side of a vast ravine. When people came to see where this had happened, the miraculousness of his survival unfolded. The other side of the ravine was considerably higher than the take-off point—An example of God's almighty hand and the wings of angels.

A mission house at the station in Ilboru on Mt. Meru was available, so we were on the move again. Before leaving Marangu, I must tell you about Martha.

Martha

Martha came along with several other women. Word had been circulated at church that the new missionary mama was looking for help. As we were beginning our ministry at the school, setting up house and caring for our three small children was more than I could handle. She stood apart from the younger women, watching as I struggled with interviews in Swahili while trying to manage our little ones. Her demeanor was of quiet dignity as she came forward with a curtsy.

"My name is Martha."

"You speak English!" I exclaimed.

"A little," she replied.

As Martha walked toward me, I noticed she had a tilted gait.

"Will you find work painful or difficult?" I inquired. She assured me that her hip dislocation was from birth and gave her no pain. Martha then reached to take the baby from my arms. He nestled quietly against her. Her smile of love and understanding left me no doubt as to whom I would choose. The two toddlers who had been hiding behind my skirt confirmed the choice by returning her smile. Martha joined our family.

Martha remained with us for eight years. Countless stories could be told of her wisdom and loving help. One of the many lessons she taught me came through an experience shared after one year together. The church had given us a new assignment, and we needed to move. Helpful students came to load our packed barrels onto a truck on moving day. Our house was located at the top of a long, steep hill, and at the base was a retaining wall. As Martha and I came out of the house with more loads, we were dismayed to see that Steve, our ever-adventurous three year old, had climbed onto the truck and was happily jumping from barrel to barrel. Dismay turned to horror as the truck began to move. The hand brake had released, and the driverless truck gained momentum down the hill with Steve bravely hanging on to the jostling barrels. A student leapt onto the truck bed, grabbed Steve and jumped off moments before the truck plunged over the retaining wall.

As Steve was returned to my arms, unharmed, I struggled to quell the hysteria of my mind: visions of seeing his small body crushed and of all the other terrifying possibilities that might have happened. Martha gently enfolded us in her arms and then proceeded to gather all the students and workers for a service of thanksgiving. Her message to me will be remembered always: "Mama, don't focus on things that might have happened, but rather rejoice and give thanks for God's loving protection."

One of the difficult lessons I needed to learn was not to grieve over leaving friends. I was given grace to deal with parting from parents and family, perhaps because of the excitement and anticipation of going to Africa. It seemed to me that, with each new friendship in our new world, came the time to say goodbye. These new friends would not be lost; we would be parted only for a time. I soon learned to value the opportunities of meeting new people and being thankful for the countless ways each one added to my life.

Our beloved Martha came with us and lived with us for eight years. It is almost impossible to list the ways she loved and cared for us. She was truly a second mother to our children and a friend to me.

When we moved to Loliondo, she moved to Nkoranga, which is not far from Arusha, where Bill and Lynn Smith had lived. It is on the foothills of Mt. Meru, as you drive from Arusha to Moshi. Here she began an orphanage. The children there were very fortunate to have someone like Martha.

Martha (left) and me with the orphans at Nkoranga

Chapter Five

Ilboru Years

Ilboru

The mountains, Kilimanjaro and Meru, are only about fifty miles from each other. Both mountains are extinct volcanoes; the lava produced thousands of years ago has made their foothills rich and productive. Having grown up in North Dakota, I have come to love the mountains, just as I have loved the prairies.

Mt Meru, 14,980 ft , from the back yard of our present day house

The mission station at Ilboru, on the foothills of Mt Meru, was begun by Germans. They built strong, livable houses, as well as churches and schools. We found all of this waiting for us as we moved into the red brick house at Ilboru. Later, we were to meet Pastor Patzig who had built and lived in this house, another connection story.

Again we were welcomed by the mission family at this lovely station: Marilyn and Stew Carlson, the headmaster at the secondary school; Pastor Bob and Esther Johnson, our dear friends from seminary and Fairview days; and Mabel Larson, who taught English and was remembered fondly by all her students. One was Anzamen Lema, who later became a director in Lutheran World Federation. The house was similar to the one we lived in at Marangu, and we fit in comfortably. Our children were thrilled to find new friends in both the mission and African families. A primary school and church were right next to us; both became a very meaningful part of our lives. The secondary school was just across the stream that ran through the compound.

Our new address was a box number in the post office of Arusha, the center of government for this area of Tanganyika. Arusha was a beautiful town, with streets lined with jacaranda trees, a central roundabout in the shopping area with a clock tower. A sign board announced that Arusha is midway between Cape Town and Cairo. Five streets filtered into this roundabout,

Arusha town center from clock tower looking to Mt. Meru

Our red brick house at Ilboru

and in giving directions we would say which street to take from the clock tower.

When we lived in a remote area of Tanzania, our connection to the rest of the world was by radio. The operator was situated in a room at the post office, facing the clock tower. Teressa not only handled all our radio calls, but also from her vantage point over the clock tower, was able to observe all that went around the roundabout. People would call and ask Teressa if so-and-so was in town, and she would reply, "They just went around about a half hour ago. I think they're having tea with so-and-so at the New Arusha Hotel."

Dave settled us into our house at Ilboru, then needed to be back in Nabarera immediately. This was a pattern of life that was a challenge to both of us, as he would often be gone two or three weeks at a time. We had no means of communication at this time, so my role was often that of a single mom. I do not remember that I ever resented this, though there were times when daddy would have certainly helped. We were able to buy a Ford Anglia and this was a great help in getting around.

One memorable afternoon a dearly-loved missionary, Elmer Danielson, who was our "spiritual head" and his wife, Lillian, had come for afternoon tea. We were sitting in the living room when little Nathan came into the room and excitedly announced, "Mommy, Mommy Uncle Dave is here!" I could see Elmer's eyes open wide. Uncle?? We welcomed Dave home and continued our tea. Afterwards, Elmer asked Dave to take a walk with him. Dave returned with a subdued look. Elmer and Lillian prayed with us and left. Later Dave told me that Elmer had thanked him for all the work he was doing and then added, "When your children think you are only an 'uncle,' perhaps you should give more time to your family." It was a tough but helpful bit of advice. He continued to put God's work first, but gave us a fair share, too.

Our family adapted to Ilboru very quickly. We had a large lawn with a garden area as well. Petro joined us and began planting the garden with a good assortment of vegetables. He enjoyed our active Steve, Naomi, and Nathan, and they enjoyed riding on his shoulders and grabbing his long earlobes like reins. The Maasai sometimes pierced the ears of their children and extended the lobes, considered a thing of beauty. Our

Petro holding Nathan and Naomi

little ones delighted in holding on to them. What a patient man our Petro was! In recent years he walks with his granddaughter to come see us, bringing gifts of vegetables, and we share a cup of chai and stories of long ago.

A large guava tree grew in our front yard, perfect for climbing. When the fruit was ready, we always knew where to find the children. Naomi had a special fondness for guavas (*mapera*) and to this day would claim them to be her favorite fruit. She would still be climbing into *mapera* trees today if her brothers had not admonished her to act a little more dignified and not embarrass them.

As we were to celebrate our first Christmas at Ilboru, we were wakened to a surprise. A long line of mothers and children were singing outside. When we went to thank them, they put their hands out and asked for their "Christmas." No one had told us of this tradition, started by the Germans, and I was totally unprepared. I only had a bag of sweets we had purchased for our children. They seemed disappointed, and I felt so bad. So many lessons I needed to learn! Dave rescued me by speaking to them, telling them of the story of the real gift of Christmas.

As we waited for child number four, I talked to Steve, Naomi, and Nathan about this gift from God. I let them feel the baby as she moved and said, "This will be our African baby." Steve and Naomi were born in America, and Nathan in England. This child would be born in Africa. How excited we all were when Rebecca Marie arrived on February 7, 1958, at the British-run, Mt. Meru Hospital in Arusha. Gwen Hiskins, a lovely mid-wife, did

Our adorable Rebecca

the honors, and all went well. After six days of pampering by the staff, Dave brought us home to the eager children. When Steve saw Rebecca, he looked at me with a hurt and angry face, "You promised us an African baby, and this one looks just like us!" A bit of explanation followed, and he became the best big brother ever.

At the beginning of our second term, we were blessed with our fifth child. Jonathan Paul was born on June 12, 1961. He was a robust red-head who delighted all. An amusing incident happened during the delivery. The doctor attending exclaimed as the head presented itself, "Oh I say! We have a little sandy!" I almost stopped pushing, because I thought I might be delivering a dog; we had a Golden Cocker Spaniel named Sandy.

Once again I was nursing a baby and devoted myself to that. Naomi claimed Jon as her baby and even though she was only six years old, she would tie him onto her back with a *kanga* (decorative material) and carry him around like the Tanzanian mamas did with their babies.

Also, around the time Jonathan was born, I received a letter from a Nordby cousin, Jeannette, who I had never met. She had just become a widow, after nursing her husband with tuberculosis for many years and was feeling directed to come see me. When she got off the plane, I was expecting a grief-stricken, haggard-looking woman. But out stepped this absolutely gorgeous woman, with men tripping over themselves trying to be of service to her. That was my cousin?! Wow! We bonded right away and have been close ever since. With her black hair, she looked more like someone related to Dave than to me. We all loved her, and she fit into our family and lifestyle right away. She called baby Jonathan, "Jon-a-bon," and that name stuck for many years. The kids called her, "Auntie Jet," and they still do.

Dave was reaching many new areas in Maasailand, as well as on the mountain among the WaArusha, an agricultural tribe with the same culture and language as the pastoral Maasai. This meant we saw him more, which was great.

Many "connections" were made during our years at Ilboru, and I would be remiss if I failed to tell of yet another lasting friendship with several links.

One day in 1961, as I was working in our garden, a taxi pulled up in the playground just on the other side of our hedge. I watched as a young couple with two small kids and lots of luggage were deposited. They were looking around and obviously were not

Auntie Jet holding baby Jonathan 1961

sure where to go, so I quickly ran out and introduced myself to them. I invited them in, and this was the beginning of this wonderful "connection."

Shoonie (Charlotte) and Gerry Hartwig had signed up to teach at the Ilboru Lutheran Secondary School on this big mission station. They were St. Olaf graduates, and we found several friends we had in common. Kris and Karl (just an infant at the time) would become playmates of our kids in the years ahead. A daughter, Kari, was born in Arusha in 1963. They left in 1964 to return to the States where Gerry would pursue his Ph.D studies at Indiana University. We kept in touch. Kurt, their fourth child, was born in Indiana just before they moved to Duke University in Durham, North Carolina. They returned to Tanzania briefly in 1968-69, when Gerry was doing research.

It was in Durham where the first tragedy struck. Karl, their second child, was killed in 1977 at the age of sixteen in a car accident.

The Hartwigs moved to Northfield, Minnesota, where Shoonie's mom lived (a couple streets from where we lived on furloughs two and three). Gerry was teaching at St. Olaf when the second tragedy struck. In 1980 Gerry suffered a heart attack while teaching and died. So much sorrow for Shoonie and her dear children! The family came back to Tanzania in 1981 to visit. First son Kristopher was about to enter medical school, and Shoonie was exploring a possible partnership between the University of Dar es Salaam and Lutheran schools, a partnership

The Hartwigs in Arusha, 2009. Left to right: Rebecca (formerly Smith), Kari, Shoonie, Nathan (son of Rebecca and Kris), Kristopher

which did indeed come to fruition and which continues to function today. Dave and Shoonie spent many hours at our table planning this project.

At the time of this visit, our goddaughter, Rebecca Smith (daughter of long-time friends Bill and Lynn Smith), came out to spend the summer with us. A friendship began as she and Kris met. We had a big yellow tree swing where the two learned to know each other and recall their lives as young children here. It was a perfect match; Kris and Rebecca were married. What a "connection" between our families! In 1988 they returned to Tanzania with three daughters. Kris worked as a doctor at a Mennonite hospital in Shirati, in the Mara Region. They stayed there until 1994, and their only Tanzania-born child, Nathan, arrived in 1993.

Shoonie has come back many times. From 1995 to 2000 she served as a missionary for the Evangelical Lutheran Church in America, starting a program called *Mwangaza*, which works to upgrade the quality of Tanzanian teachers. The headquarters for this organization is at Ilboru, so we have seen her often. In 2004, Kris and Rebecca returned to start up the hospice program at Selian Lutheran Hospital with Paulina Natema, a wonderful young lady who I mentored at the age of fifteen working in the Maternal Child Healthcare clinics. They lived in a house just on the other side of our hedge; both Kris and Rebecca have taken such good care of us as we go through one medical crisis after another. Such countless acts of loving care! They are included as part of our family for many occasions and stop in for chai now and then. Their son, Nathan, and our grandson, Luke, have become very close friends. The "connections" continue.

Mama Mesiaki

In the Maasai tradition, parents are often called by the name of their first child. Dave answered to Baba Stefano, for our first son, Stephen, while I was called by the name of our first daughter, Mama Naomi. I only knew Mama Mesiaki by this name, and it was only when she died at the age of 120 years that I finally learned her given name: Natabubkoki, which means "she who has received salvation." She was my salvation in so many ways.

In 1957, we were transferred from our one-year posting at Marangu Teachers Training College on Mt. Kilimanjaro to the mission station in Ilboru, on Mt. Meru, where Dave would begin his work among the Maasai in the vast area south of Arusha.

One of the first Tanzanian women to welcome us to the Ilboru area was Mama Mesiaki, an energetic mama who helped lead the Maasai in Christian outreach. The Maasai Christians,

Mama Mesiaki shaking hands with a political dignitary

along with the four mission families associated with the secondary school, formed a wonderful and supportive group. This African congregation became a large part of our lives. Mama Mesiaki was always bringing new women to meet me, and when they learned I was a nurse, my role in their lives took a dramatic change in direction. They began to bring their sick children to me at our home and, with limited resources, I treated them or took them in my little car to the government hospital. One of my frustrations in these situations was that my Kiswahili was barely existent, but love always found its own language and bound us together.

One day an eight-year old boy was brought to me in a serious state. He had fallen against a barbed-wire fence and had slashed his throat. This was the first real emergency I had faced, and had it not been for the ever-present Mama Mesiaki, my faithful Martha, and God answering our prayers, getting this boy to the hospital where his life was saved may not have had the positive ending we experienced.

Mama Mesiaki asked me one day, as she watched me sewing a dress for our three year old, Naomi, "Would you be willing to teach sewing to the ladies?" That began yet another bond with these dear Maasai women. We would share God's word over our cloth, patterns, and sewing needles as we met each Wednesday at our home. I can't say I was exactly the Martha Stewart of design, but God always seemed to give me the appropriate words and strategies needed to complete the task.

I learned to admire Mama Mesiaki even more as I learned her story. She had been in the first group of Maasai who had received Christ and had been baptized. Her husband had taken a second wife, which was against Mama Mesiaki's Christian beliefs, but within Maasai tribal custom. Rather than treating the younger woman badly, Mama Mesiaki welcomed her with Christian love, and through all the years I knew her she lived near her husband and his other wife, but alone in her own hut. She had several children, starting with her eldest, Mesiaki. With her strong faith, she brought these children up in the love of the Lord. Mesiaki became a pastor and later the first president of the newly-formed Arusha/Maasai Synod. Dave and Mesiaki became like brothers, and through the many years that followed our friendship with the family of Mama Mesiaki grew.

In the late 1960s, there was a serious outbreak of hepatitis, and much of my time was spent in caring for the sick. I foolishly ignored my own symptoms until I collapsed and was taken to the Lutheran hospital in Machame, on the slopes of Mt. Kilimanjaro. Two German doctors lovingly cared for me, but after a month of gastric tubes, IVs and countless medications, I received the news that my liver was permanently damaged. I would need to limit my activities for the rest of my life. By this time Dave and I had five children who needed me, plus there were many areas of our mission relying on my continued involvement. How would I cope?

Returning home, I found myself discouraged and depressed. Our dear Martha had been of immeasurable help to Dave in caring for our children. Friends brought food and tried to comfort me, yet I felt so useless. Among the many that came was dear Mama Mesiaki. Each day she would ask God, "Who needs my help this day?" Such was her relationship with her Lord, that she would ask and God would answer. She would fill her basket with whatever she felt was needed, always including her Bible and hymn book. She came to me one day when I was very weak and discouraged. "God told me to bring healing to you today," she announced. She then asked me if I believed in healing. "That I'm alive is a miracle," I told her. "Yes," she agreed, but she continued to ask if I truly believed God could heal my liver completely. "God's will be done. I believe," I said.

Mama Mesiaki then reached into her basket and took out a jar of Vick's Vapor Rub. She explained that she didn't have anything else appropriate, but that God could anoint with this. She unscrewed the cap, dipped her fingers into the aromatic balm, and spread the salve on my skin above my liver. She then laid her hands on me with prayer, thanking God for the healing that God had done. I felt the warmth of the Vicks combined with the warmth of her hands. During the silence that followed the prayers, my mood lifted and I felt a sense of peace. After this sober rite, in her no-nonsense way, she left quickly, saying God had put someone else on her list.

When I was strong enough to travel, we took our furlough to the States. My cousin, Jeannette (Auntie Jet), who had lived with us in Arusha, was now married to a renowned radiologist, Dr. Leslie Bakos. They were living in British Columbia, Canada. He was very curious to have me tested for liver damage. After many tests, he shook his head and asked, "Are you sure you've had hepatitis? Your liver is in perfect condition."

Ashe Ngai (Maa), *Asante Mungu* (KiSwahili)—Thank you God! And bless you, Mama Mesiaki!

After many years, Mama Mesiaki could no longer walk to those on her list, but her witness continued until her death at 120 years of age!

Siafu

Our years at Ilboru were filled with many interesting "connections." Some brightened our lives for a short time, while so many have been lasting. We were blessed with so many visitors; to list them all would take too much time. Some visits stand out because they were very memorable.

The man known as Mr. Lutheran, Bishop Franklin Clark Fry, and his lovely wife were visiting the work of the church in Tanzania. Somehow, I was to have a reception for them at our house. We missionary women planned who would bring what, so my responsibilities were shared by all. Excitement about having this distinguished elder, ran high. We women all wanted to look our best, as well as share our culinary goodies.

The afternoon arrived and all was ready. My dining room table had never looked better, with all the food, candles, and flowers. Our husbands would introduce each family (everyone hoping the kids would behave) and then we would share food.

Our house was filled, and there was not enough room for everyone to move about comfortably, so some bright man suggested we move everything to our spacious (but not recently mowed) front lawn. This was done with many helping hands, and the serving began.

Unbeknownst to us, an army of *siafu* had moved into the entire front yard. These flesh-eating ants had cursed many an occasion; they climb up one's legs until something blocks their way. Then they bite and hang on fiercely. What happened next would make the funniest movie imaginable. We women in our lovely gowns and the men in their fancy suits began grabbing ourselves in the most unseemly manner. Bishop Fry and his wife nearly dropped their laden plates, looking around to understand what was attacking them. I brought them into our guest room and advised them to take off their clothes and pull those ants off. Others were trying to find a tree or bush to hide behind. The women came running into the house, and the kids were screaming. As this wild activity was happening, God added his final surprise—a sudden downpour. Clothes and fancy hairdos were spoiled, the lovely food was soaked, and the pain of bites and embarrassment was intense.

Then, when most of the ants had been picked off, we sodden missionaries together with the Frys, gathered. I believe it was an equalizing experience orchestrated by God to remind us that we are all the same, and there was no need for anyone to be hoity toity. We all had a good laugh!

Patzig

Our Ilboru house held many special memories for all who lived in it before us. It was built by German missionaries in the early 1900s, as they established a station with church, schools, and homes for their people. These people built well and built to last, using stone and brick. The house was two stories, with two bedrooms, a kitchen, a living room, and a dining room. Earlier occupants had added on a storeroom and a veranda, and we added another bedroom and a toilet/bath.

I often wondered about the lives of those who had begun the great kingdom work here. Their names were spoken with great respect by those first Maasai Christians. The First World War brought a sudden end to their work. As the victorious British army took over Tanganyika, these families were given only a few hours to gather their belongings before they were taken to camps.

One day, in our second term in this house, we received a letter from the pastor who had been one of the first to work in Ilboru and the first to live in this house. He was in his eighties and wanted once more to see the station where he and his family had lived. Pastor Patzig asked if he could come to be with us. We had a small guest house that was prepared for him. It would be a humble dwelling, but he could eat and be with us as he wished.

We had spread the word around Ilboru that he was coming. Many remembered him and asked to have him come visit. His return and reception was touching. This small-in-stature but large-in-presence man warmed our hearts immediately. Our children gave him the name, "Grandpa Pepsi." Pastor Patzig's time with us went quickly, and we felt sad when he said that he had to leave. He had one request which seemed very strange: could he go upstairs? We had made a room for our Martha up there, and the remainder was like any attic, filled with barrels and boxes. Dave was on safari, and the children were away playing with friends, so I was the only one to witness the reason for his trip to the attic. He came down carrying a foot-long metal box, rusted and covered with dust. I cleared a place on the dining table and covered it with paper. He explained that the day he and his family were forced to leave, he gathered important papers and photos and hid them somewhere. He never told me where, but this box was just where he had hidden it. None of the several families who livied in the house after him had ever found it.

I sensed this was a very painful moment for him, so I said I would leave. He asked me to stay. The first item he took from the box was a photo of his wife, who had died shortly before he came to us. This photo was part of his reason for wanting to return. He held it to his heart and then drew out another photo—his only son, who had been killed in the war. My tears fell with his, and my heart felt such a special bond with him. There were certificates and many papers that I did not need to know about, but the memory of that special day can still bring tears to my eyes.

Our friendship with Patzig continued on our furlough trip to the States. He invited us to stop at his house near Munich. His daughter gave us such a warm welcome, telling us how thankful her father had been to have stayed with us.

At the age of ninety, he returned to Tanganyika again for the dedication of the church he had built in Kimandolu, to which Dave had built the extension and pulpit. What joy to see that great man in the pulpit, greeting all in Maa, the language of the Maasai!

Arusha School

The final years of our first five-year term were full of new learning experiences for all of us. Dave was fully absorbed in his work with the Maasai. My days were filled with mothering, learning languages and customs, as well as women's work—Bible studies, sewing, and medical care. The children adapted quickly to this land and people; they had known no other. Their friends were the other mission kids as well as the African children. We lived adjacent to the primary school, and our children joined in their recess times and even sat in on some of their lessons.

On our first furlough in Moorhead, Minnesota, Stephen started first grade and Naomi attended kindergarten at Good Shepherd Lutheran Church.

Stephen (standard 2) and Naomi (standard 1) were the first of our children to attend the British primary school in Arusha, starting there when we returned from furlough. It was a beautifully built school, with a proper headmaster and great teachers. We fitted Stephen out in the school uniform—khaki shorts, bottle green shirt, grey knee-high socks, black shoes, and a grey felt hat. Naomi's uniform was similar, except that she wore a bottle green dress. We were cautioned that the African sun could be damaging to the child's mind and a hat should be worn whenever outside. Like everything in his life, this was a new adventure for Stephen. Naomi always seemed to get in on the adventures, too. The Carlson family had children of school age, so we took turns bringing them and collecting them. My favorite memory was a day when Stephen proudly recited a poem learned at school. He stood very straight, looked forward, and began in a totally British accent:

> *One misty, moisty morning,* (pronounced "mawh-ning")
> *When cloudy was the weather,* (pronounced "wetha")
> *I chanced* ("ch-awe-nced") *to see an old man,*
> *Clothed all in leather* ("clo-thed" all in "letha")

It still makes me smile each time I remember and mimic him.

The next year, Nathan joined the others. All acquired a British accent and many good table manners. They had lunch each day in a strictly supervised dining room. One evening our rowdy group was behaving badly, and I asked, "Could you show me how you sit for lunch at school?" Thinking it was a game, they straightened their chairs, at a proper distance from the table, arranged their dishes and silverware according to English patterns, placed their hand in their laps, and politely asked, "Please, would you pass the food." Only then did they eat—with fork in the left hand and knife in the right (the opposite for Nate as our "lefty'). This caused total amazement on my behalf and a rising feeling of admiration for the British.

Becky's first year of school was in Northfield, Minnesota, on our second furlough year. When we returned to Ilboru, she attended Arusha School for one year, then joined the older three at the Lutheran boarding school in Kiomboi in central Tanzania.

An interesting "connection" happened when Steve was in Standard 2. Marilyn (although, she was always called "Honey"), the daughter of dear friends, Dr. Roy and Betty Shaffer, came to school. She told us years later, when she was engaged to Steve, that he was feared by all the little girls because he would chase them to capture a kiss!

The Shaffer Connection

Many "connections" made during our first term have remained strong and been reinforced up to today.

One of these "connections" began when Dave and others working with the Maasai people heard about a missionary family in Kenya who worked with the Maasai. Roy and Ruth Shaffer were with the Africa Inland Mission, stationed in Loitokitok on Mt. Kilimanjaro. Ruth Shaffer was a gifted linguist and had written a Maasai grammar. Would she be willing to come and teach these men?

Ruth Shaffer came and lived with us for several weeks, becoming a dear part of our family. She had a strong personality, which our little ones recognized and honored. One day when they were being troublesome, Ruth said, "The Bible says you can B-E-A-T a child with a R-O-D and he will not D-I-E." I could never see her doing that.

Bill Jacobson, Elder Jackson, and Bill Smith joined the Maasai sessions, and all appreciated this amazing woman. They would sit together in our front yard, where the commotion of a lively household would not interrupt. Several Maasai were brought in as well; some good connections began there.

Ruth and Roy were retiring and plans were made to move to a retreat community in Florida. Ruth invited Dave to come visit them there and continue the studies. This kind invitation was accepted with thanks, and plans were made for his going to Florida with Bill Smith in January 1960, when we would be on furlough in Moorhead, Minnesota.

Winter was such a new experience for the children, who had known only tropical weather all their lives. Having Dave leave for Florida sunshine seemed a little unfair, but we entered into snow activities with great enthusiasm. My reward was to fly to Florida at the end of their studies, then come back with Dave by train.

The women of our Moorhead neighborhood were excited for me and decided this could be a second honeymoon, so they put on a shower of sexy lingerie for me. I asked my parents to come stay with the children. I bought my airplane ticket and counted the days.

Just a couple of days before my departure date, Naomi came down with mumps, and my father had an emergency in his congregation, so they informed us that they would be a day late in coming. I was able to change my ticket until the following day.

The Electra airplane on which I should have been flying exploded over Indiana. There were no survivors. Phone calls poured in from family and friends who thought I was on that flight. It was a time of thankfulness and wonder that God had spared me. The next day's flight was frightening. As we neared Tampa, we were caught in a wild storm and very nearly crashed.

Needless to say, I was not the eager "bride" on arrival, but an emotional wreck. A few days of Dave, sunshine, time with the Shaffers, and our great friends, Bill and Lynn Smith, restored me quickly. Parting from the Shaffers may have seemed the end of a wonderful connection, but God had other plans to keep this strong.

Just a note to conclude this Florida holiday: I became

Lynn and Bill Smith

ill on our last day there. On the long train ride back to Minneapolis, where a party was planned for us, my neck and chin swelled up. Mumps. Not a nice disease for grownups, especially with a large group of family and friends waiting to see you. By the time we reached Moorhead the next day, I was very ill, as were the kids. Becky and Steve had mumps. My parents needed to leave, and Dave was scheduled to speak in another state. It was not the happiest moment in my life.

But, to continue the Simonson–Shaffer connection: The Shaffers had a son, Roy, who had grown up in Kenya and married Betty Lane after completing his studies at Wheaton College. Our "connection" to this great family continued when Roy was a doctor and wished to return to East Africa. At that time Dave was working in Monduli, a Maasai center near Arusha. There was an opening for a medical officer, and the position was offered to Roy, through African Medical and Research Foundation in Nairobi. Our families meshed in a marvelous way.

In reminiscing with Roy in later years, he told me of playing rugby on a Monduli team with the district officer, a Mr. Stevenson, against Dave on the Arusha team.

Betty and I shared some early "connections" during those early months after they came to Monduli. She was expecting their sixth child and, because of placenta-previa, she required a c-section. For this, she was brought into Arusha. Four of their children were in boarding school in Arusha and the youngest, Betsy, came to be with us. Roy was in the midst of a big medical research program and needed to leave after the birth of Ginny. Betty and I bonded as sisters when she came to stay with us. She

 had a difficult time, and I was so thankful for being a part of her recovery. Jonathan was just a toddler at the time and as Betty observed his

Shaffer family in Nairobi 1967 Front - Marilyn, Betty, Betsy, Roy, and Ginnny. Back - David, Carolyn, and Dan

many boyish antics she exclaimed, "Thank goodness we had a girl!"

We had so many shared experiences during the Shaffers' Monduli/Arusha years. They moved to Nairobi. One vacation, we decided that our two families should do a safari together, from Nairobi through Maasailand to Loliondo in northern Tanzania, to visit Stan and Marie Benson. With their six children and our five, we were quite a crew. The kids kept changing cars with every potty stop we made in the bushes. We had made a more civilized potty break at Narok, on the border between Kenya and Tanzania, where friends of the Shaffers lived on a mission station. They kindly invited us to use their facilities. After visiting, everyone piled back into the LandRovers, and we headed back on the road. The rains had been heavy, and the soil was "black cotton," so traveling was slow and we kept getting stuck, with everyone piling out to help push. When we had gone for about an hour and were all getting back into the vehicles, some wise person said, "Let's take roll call!" We kept coming up one short. Lo and behold, little four-year-old Becky had been left behind. It was back through the mud to the mission. There was Becky, being well cared for by the missionary lady, who had assured Becky that we would be coming back for her. She had gone into the bathroom when we had decided to leave. We were happy to be reunited, and we once again continued on.

We were welcomed to Loliondo by the Bensons and immediately told them the Becky story. She began to feel very special; when we returned to Arusha and related this story, she would just shine. If I failed to tell the story to someone, she would tug on my skirt and say, "Tell them the story."

The Shaffers moved back to the States, and we visited them in New York on one of our furloughs. Our children went on to college. When their daughter, Marilyn, completed her studies at Wheaton College and Steve was already back in Tanzania, working with Lutheran World Relief, our families connected again in a special way. Marilyn came to the International School in Moshi as a French teacher. She spent many weekends with our family, and that naughty, kissing second-grader from Arusha School days fell in love with "Honey."

Roy and Betty were back in Nairobi; their son David and his wife joined Marilyn in Moshi at the International School, so the

Steve and Marilyn's wedding in Arusha. Left to right—Naomi, Rebecca, Ginny, Betsy, Samantha Lister, Marilyn, Steve, Nathan, David, Jonathan, Dan

Shaffer–Simonson network broadened. Later her sister, Carolyn, came to the International School as well.

Operation Bootstrap Africa

Tanganyika gained independence in 1962, and a new era of excitement and challenge began. It was a peaceful transition, for which we thanked God. Kenya had achieved independence after years of Mau Mau terror. Word had reached Tanganyikans that some of those terrorists were waiting to disrupt and bring trouble. The night of independence, Dave and others from Ilboru Secondary School patrolled the area but met no intruders.

Julius Nyerere was elected the first president. He came from a small tribe and had been educated in Tanganyika and England. *Mwalimu* (teacher) was the name or title given to him, as he had the gifts of a visionary and taught as he spoke and led. The man he appointed as secretary of education was Solomon Eliofoo—a man Dave had come to know well at the University of London. This wonderful "connection" was again renewed. Dave was called to Dar es Salaam to meet with Solomon.

"How can I best help this new nation?" Dave asked.

"We must have schools. The children must receive education," replied Eliofoo.

A new challenge was laid for Dave, and together they came up with a plan. The paramount basics for this program, which Dave felt his friends in America would support, was that of self-help and dignity. The old cowboy slogan, of lifting ones self up by ones bootstraps, was how Dave saw this program. Operation Bootstrap came into being, as Dave presented it to churches and friends in America. A school would be requested by the people in a village and was approved by the Community Development Trust Fund under the Ministry of Education. The people themselves would do all the manual labor—making bricks, hauling water—and the materials would be supplied by Operation Bootstrap. These schoolrooms needed to be built to a high standard, and so were supervised by accredited builders.

The response of churches and individuals was thrilling. Many came together, and a certified board was formed. Very many great people made this all happen. I fear to single out any other than Deana Miller, who for thirty years kept this ever-expanding program going. Operation Bootstrap Africa has gone beyond classrooms (over 3,000 built in Tanzania) and also now works in several countries and handles school sponsorships for Maasai girls at the Maasai Girls Lutheran Secondary School in Monduli.

I will never forget the visit we had with *Mwalimu* Nyerere. He had invited us and several visiting Operation Bootstrap Africa board members to the State House in Dar es Salaam, for tea. He was dressed simply, in a short-sleeved sports shirt and white

Gladys and Rudolph Simonson at OBA banquet with sons James, Paul, Luther and David

trousers. He put us all at ease, with his great smile. He had invited us, to thank Dave personally for Operation Bootstrap Africa and also to thank the Madsens from the States. He shared with passion his dreams of an educated people. As we relaxed and drank our tea, the conversation also relaxed. At that point, he placed his hand on my knee and asked, "What are you doing for our country?" To this day, I cannot recall my answer, but he thanked me with a sincere handshake. Another treasured memory!

CHAPTER SIX

Years in Exile

The Dismissal

As we neared the end of our second term, our lives seemed to be filled with many interesting and challenging projects. We were being accepted by the people of the plains and of the mountains. In fact, Dave had been made a true elder in the Maasai tribe, in an emotional ceremony. I specify "true" elder, because his position was beyond that of an honorary member, as it gave him voting rights within the tribe.

As we were approaching the departure for our second furlough, plans for so many projects were already being made for our return in a year's time. The Arusha/ Maasai people, had given us a very beautiful piece of land on a foothill of Mount Meru where they intended for us to live and work until God called us home. We felt so secure and excited about the future.

Then a summons came from the African bishop, Stephano Moshi. Dave was to meet with the bishop. At that point in time, all of northern Tanzania was under the leadership of this bishop, who was from the Chagaa tribe, located on Mount Kilimanjaro. Dave went and returned with the bishop's decision that we were no longer needed and would not return. I was never told the reasons given for this dismissal, but Dave's look of shock and anguish spoke volumes. Why? What had we done? All of these questions came through tears and disbelief.

Dave shared this with several pastors, and the word spread like the wind. People came to embrace and comfort me. The men would not accept this decision. Groups were organized. Petitions were circulated and signed. Delegations from many congregations carried these petitions to Moshi and presented them to the bishop. We learned that one of the bishop's main concerns was that a new diocese would be formed if Dave was allowed to continue. This became a threat the people sensed, and they told the bishop that if he did not agree to our return, they would separate. Only when the oldest elder confronted the bishop with the words, "Simonson will return. Do you hear me?" *"Unanisikia Baba?"* was the bishop forced to listen. This eldest elder was one age-class above the bishop, so when he pointed his finger at the bishop and said these words, the decision was reversed. The respect of the African people for those of an older age group is awesome.

To save face, the bishop said that we would be sent to the most remote area of Maasailand, where Dave would not have the influence on the people. The ironic thing was that Dave had not been encouraging the people to separate but, rather, had spoken openly and boldly on their behalf when he knew they were not receiving some of the support designated for them.

Jubilation, thanksgiving, and renewed enthusiasm filled our hearts. Wherever we were sent, it would be wonderful, because we were back where our hearts felt called.

In reading the book, *Loyalty*, a biography of Richard Reusch, there was a paragraph about the dismissal. Bishop Moshi was recorded as saying, "When being charged by an elephant, one is wise to move out of the way and let the elephant pass. Simonson will go to Loliondo without any financial support."

Loliondo

Even the name, Loliondo, sounds like the area—rolling hills that made me say,-"Lo, behold the beauty of God's creation!"

We had visited this beautiful area of northern Tanzania, when Stan and Marie Benson had served there. And now we were to spend our third term of four years there. It was exciting and a great relief to reach the town of Loliondo, after packing our earthly possessions and five children into our old LandRover and crossing the vast Serengeti plains. This twelve-hour drive was always exciting because of the amazing things to be seen along the way. We passed through areas of cultivation—bananas, coffee, and wheat—then ascended and circled on the rim of the famous Ngorongoro Crater, and descended to the Serengeti. What people from all over the world come to see, we saw regularly when we brought the children to their boarding schools. We never tired of seeing vast herds of animals—zebra, wildebeest, gazelle, elephants, and often lions, leopards, and cheetahs.

Our stone house, built by missionary Bill Jacobson, with additions by Stan, was nestled against the side of a hill. It was immediately home to us. We were warmly welcomed by the evangelist and many others.

The town was a government center for this northern area, with a few offices, a primary school, the Catholic mission, our Lutheran church, and a short row of *dukas* (shops), run by several families of the Singh community (Sikhs). It didn't take long to become acquainted with everyone there.

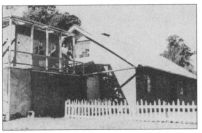

Our Loliondo house with Dave standing by his office, built on top of the cistern

It took very little time to settle into this new place. The basic furniture of beds, chairs, tables, and a wood-burning stove were in place. As we added our bits and pieces, it felt like home.

Stan Benson had built an office above the cistern (our water supply). Dave unpacked his books on the shelves and his typewriter on the desk; he was ready. Not that

The Sisters (medical nuns) at Wasso Hospital

he spent much time there, he was out familiarizing himself with the people. We had been sent here with no budget for travel, so Dave would walk the many miles to reach the Maasai and Sonjo villages. I often did these walks with him. One of our favorite walks was the five miles to a village called Wasso. The Catholics had a small hospital, run by four wonderful and dedicated sisters (medical nuns) from Austria. Through the four years in Loliondo, I became very attached to these dear women and the Austrian doctor, Father Watchinger.

A large airstrip had been built near Wasso and, because I had been working with the Flying Doctor Service while in Arusha, I was invited to assist them when the doctors came for their monthly visits to do surgery. I have shared some of these medical adventures in other stories. This airstrip was well maintained and used by government as well as tourists. One interesting occasion came one day when a plane buzzed our house, so Dave felt he was needed at the airstrip and drove immediately there. The pilot, who knew Dave, explained he had four German tourists who had some connection to the church in Loliondo and wished to be taken there. Would David be willing to help him with this request? The well-dressed couples were very grateful, and Dave brought them by the house before showing them around. With no restaurants in Loliondo, I invited them for lunch after their tour. Luckily we had recently returned from Nairobi where our oldest, Steve, was in secondary school at Rift Valley Academy near Nairobi. We had done a major shopping, so I had many things to easily prepare for lunch. A tuna fish pasta salad, fruit, and freshly baked bread was our quick menu for that lunch. They were enjoying the salad and one woman said how good it was. I replied in my theatrical manner, by saying, "I owe it all to Hellmann's Mayonnaise." They looked at each other and began to laugh saying, "We are one of the Hellmann family!" The things of coincidence are such fun.

My days were filled with a variety of projects, as I became acquainted with the women of the church. There were many opportunities to teach health and Bible, both so related. I enjoyed visiting the nearby Maasai *bomas* with Dave. A delightful surprise was the visits of so many. I had thought we would be isolated from our friends in Arusha, but we were seldom without visitors. When the children were home on school vacations, they often brought friends with them. It seemed to be an adventure to hike with Dave to Sonjo (a tribe located near Lake Natron) or to the Maasai *bomas*. Our social life included a variety of

Sunday services

Dave and kids hiking to Sonjo

interesting people. The Catholic Fathers—Vince Donovan, Ned Marchessault, and Jerry Kohler—enjoyed eating with us on many occasions. During our second year there, we became very close to an American vet, Andy Clark; we even were attendants at the wedding of Andy to Barb. American Peace Corps was also a fascinating part of our life. Many stayed with us, and I joined them in their immunization programs for the people of this area. Dr. Jim Morrisey headed up several of these programs and remains a dear friend, as have many others of that time.

When we recall these years with the children, they often say, "The best years of our life." Jonathan was four years old and became very close to the children around us. Our cook and family lived in a house next to us; their two little boys were Jon's age. Their many antics were amazing. Jon was given a baby goat, which he named Wrinkles. (It was Christmas time, and he ate all the tinsel off the bottom of the tree)! We also had a terrific Rottweiler dog, Brutus, with a story all his own. The goat and dog became favorite playmates to these boys. They would dress Wrinkles and hook him up to Jon's little red wagon, which he called the Loliondo Bus.

The Loliondo gang

Jonathan and friends

As Jon neared six, we began to prepare him to go to boarding school at Kiomboi. Sending off our youngest was not easy for me, even though we knew he would be happy to be with Becky, Nathan, Naomi, and other mission children.

Becky was our animal lover—cats, rabbits, and often little rodents she could not bear to see killed. She was allowed to bring her rabbits to school. These long safaris—twelve hours to Arusha and another bus ride of ten hours to Kiomboi—were brightened for her with these dear pets. She found it difficult to leave home, but once at school she was happy. Having big brother Nathan and sister Naomi there with her was a big help too. Parents were asked to take turns chaperoning the bus, and the few times I did this, were always eventful. During the rainy season, the roads were a challenge to everyone, but the children loved getting stuck or breaking down. On one such trip, a bridge had been washed out. The man accompanying the children decided to rope the children together and cross the raging river. With bags on their backs and caged animals on their heads, these brave children found this the "best safari ever." When we parents heard the story, we were filled with thanks for their safety (and a bit angry at the risk taken).

When Nathan was ten and Steve twelve, Dave decided to make a foot safari with them, from Loliondo to Arusha. They were too young to climb Kilimanjaro, so Dave felt this 200-mile walk would be a better challenge for them. When I heard later of all they experienced, my heart nearly broke. Had I known what they were facing, I might have protested (even knowing it would not change the minds of these Simonson men). Their path was over the Sonjo Escarpment, where they hired two men to lead and help carry the loads. The volcano Oldoinyo Lengai, by which they would pass, had erupted the year before, changing many of the trails, rivers, and landmarks, so a guide was necessary. Many of the water sources were gone, and their water bottles were empty by the third day. Dave left the boys with the guides and searched and prayed. He came across a small lake of fresh water, unknown to have existed. Their stories were so amazing! Another day when the water supply was finished, Steve said, "Just strike the rock, Dad" (remembering stories of Moses in the wilderness). Again, God provided a fresh spring, unknown to exist. When I met them in Arusha, they were a pretty exhausted but proud group. Nathan's shoes had fallen apart, and he needed support to complete the walk. Both Steve and Nate have gone on to do many great things, and this was a good beginning.

First Walk: Loliondo to Arusha (as recounted by Steve)

I don't remember everything from the trip, but here are the highlights that I do remember.

Dad felt a need to do something with his boys and, because we were too young to climb Kilimanjaro, he and Barry Bloom, Peace Corps director in Tanzania, decided to walk the old cattle trail from Loliondo to Arusha. They found a Sonjo (a small tribe that hunts with poison arrows) man who said he had done it, and hired twelve or thirteen Sonjo porters. I'm not sure what they carried, as it seems to me we carried all our supplies ourselves on the first leg from Loliondo to Sonjo. Maybe we had sent a car down to Sonjo earlier. Anyway, we each—Dad, Barry, Nate, and I— had about fifty-pound packs when we left the house that day. I remember that it was a long day, too, as we went all the way to Sale, instead of just to Samunge, like we usually did. Dad, Barry, and maybe Nate, all sacked out on the school benches while I cooked up soup. I remember being full of energy and wondered why this seemed to offend Dad and Barry. Next morning the whole entourage set off for Arusha. I felt like an old missionary explorer with our long line of porters heading off across the bush. Nothing much happened that day, and it was fairly flat, short, and easy. We all slept on the ground. Early in the evening, a Sonjo let out a loud whoop and started beating his blankets. Evidently he had gone to bed with a snake.

Day three was down the Rift wall (the great Rift runs from Jordan through the eastern side of Africa to Mozambique) towards Lake Natron. The river and black volcanic rocks at Mosnik provide a strong memory because we were very hot and thirsty by the time we got there. Unfortunately, I don't think it was drinkable, but I'm not sure about that. Anyway, drinking water was about to become a major problem. We moved on to where the guide remembered a spring. He remembered correctly, and we found the spring. Unfortunately, because Oldoinyo Lengai (in Maa, "Mountain of God") had erupted recently, the spring was brackish and not drinkable. Speaking of Lengai, the whole area was coated in ash, the trees were just skeletons as were the Maasai cows, and there were no people living anywhere around.

Day four was probably the toughest of the whole hike. We set off ahead of the porters so we could make time before the sun got too hot and fried us. We got most of the way around the lake and then holed up, literally. I remember trying to squeeze in a small ledge in a river bank to get out of the sun. We waited many hours, and Dad doled out the only water we had, two canteens, a capful at a time. The porters who were carrying the water never showed up. I'm not sure if they eventually showed up and we had moved on, or if we moved on and they eventually showed up. We did make it to the other side, and all of us collapsed under a tree. It was a good thing that it was after 4:00 p.m. as the tree had no leaves. We were one big happy family under the dead tree, but both the guide and Barry had bloody shits and figured they would die there.

This must have been a pretty tough time for Dad as the walk was his idea and now it looked like everyone might die on him. I wasn't worried as I pretty much figured that Dad was God and everything would work out fine. This was later pretty much verified except that dad probably wasn't God. Rather than sit and watch everybody die or sound like they were dying, Dad took Nate and me and headed up a dry river bed in hopes of ?? We did like the elephants and started digging holes as we went up the river and sure enough, we eventually hit damp patches. We hurried up the river course and when I crested a small rise, *Kumbe*!!! (Swahili exclamation of unbelief). There was a whole lake in front of me. Not only that, it had waves on it. We hurried back to the dead tree, and everyone trucked on up to the lake to make camp. That was a really nice feeling, camping on a lake shore in the middle of the desert.

From there we began working our way around a lot of hills and eventually ended up at Gelai Bomba. I don't think we did much there but camped somewhere between Gelai and Incumbent. Memories of this section of the trip are of elephant coming down the valley towards us and then stopping by a Maasai *boma*, where the mamas all went nuts over Nate (he was little then), giving him sour milk and cussing Dad out for taking him on this safari. Another great feeling was walking into Kitumbeini and getting cold sodas at the *duka*. The height of luxury!

The next day, the porters where getting sore and started to bitch. They wanted meat! We did have a gun but saw no game. That evening as we crested a rise, we saw headlights quickly leaving. When we went to investigate, we found a freshly killed eland. I guess that poachers had shot the eland but, before they could load it, saw our entourage coming over the hill. We must have looked like game scouts—four Europeans and thirteen Africans—and they took off. Now the porters had all the meat they could eat, and Dad was starting to get a Moses complex!

The porters partied all night and the next morning, were pretty hung over, if you can get hung over on meat. Now they started grumbling about water, as they had gorged on meat and finished all the water. Even Moses had these problems. Me, I was not worried, being a man (boy) of great faith (in my father). Sure enough, by noon we came to a bubbling spring among the acacia trees. Dad didn't even have to hit it with his stick. I don't remember much after this, other than the last push into Arusha. It was dark, and we were on the Nairobi-Arusha road. Nate's shoes had ruptured and were flapping all the way into town. We had tea at Samweli's house and rode into town in a large black GM carryall.

And that is all I remember about that walk.

Naomi's Rememberances

Mom asked me to jot down some of my feelings about our time in Loliondo and other childhood memories. Here are bits and pieces of what I remember.

I was still at Kiomboi, the primary school where Lutheran missionary kids boarded and studied in central Tanzania, when we lived at Loliondo. The school year was such that we would be at school for three months, followed by one month at home, then back for three months, etc. To get home to Loliondo, we would have to ride across the Serengeti plains. The vast expanses, beautiful scenery, and abundant wildlife always made the trip wonderful—even though it took about twelve hours. I especially enjoyed these safaris home during the rains when we would often get stuck out in the boonies. I don't know what it was about rolling up my jeans and taking off my shoes, then getting behind the LandRover to push as hard as we could. The mud oozing through my toes was a delicious feeling, and then getting sprayed all over in mud flinging up from the tires caused great mirth, with giggles and squeals. Whenever we left Loliondo to head back to school, we would leave at 4:00 a.m. (Actually Dad usually started all his safaris at this ungodly hour.) We would have a picnic breakfast under a specific acacia tree on the Serengeti. It became a tradition and was a wonderful way to start the day as the sun began to rise and make shadows on the *kopjes* (granite rock outcroppings) that are scattered around on the plains.

While at Loliondo for the month vacation, I would enjoy walking through the bush about five miles to Wasso Hospital to visit the Catholic sisters. They always gave us chai and tasty homemade cookies, like those from their homeland of Austria. The Catholic priests lived in the opposite direction from our house, and we walked up there to visit. (Being a teenager, I always went with the hopes of a view of Father Ned, who was so handsome.) We would also walk to visit Barb and Andy Clark, a veterinarian from the Peace Corps, or to see Joe Strauss, also in the Peace Corps. Joe taught me how to play the guitar, and we would sit and play Beatle's songs. He was very musically talented. Occasionally we would be invited to one of the Singh's homes for curry dinner; I remember the curry being so hot tears would pour from our eyes, but then we would have lots of sodas to drink. Occasionally we would drive up into the forest on the edge of the escarpment that looked out towards Oldoinyo Lengai and Lake Natron. There were birds known as kites that would perform acrobatic stunts, flying almost eye level over where the escarpment dropped off into thin air; they were enjoying the thermals from the valley. One of their stunts was particularly funny: While one was flying right-side-up, another would fly up-side-down and grasp the other's feet. These birds kept us entertained with lots of laughter. One time, we stayed until after dark and watched as Oldoinyo Lengai erupted. Huge, red-hot boulders would shoot up into the air from the mountain— who needs fire works! It was so exciting. In general, life at Loliondo was never boring, and there was always the sense of adventures to be had and a wonderful primitive feeling of freedom. I guess this appeals to the wild child in me.

During our early years in Ilboru/Arusha, my most positive strong memory, which to this day I still crave, is spending hours every day in the *mapera* (guava) trees in our back yard. I loved climbing trees period, but when I could combine that with eating *maperas*, it was heaven. To this day the family teases me when *mapera* season comes around.

Naomi with orphan zebra

At my age I have given up climbing to get my own *maperas*; I still yearn to do so, but my brothers have asked that I not embarrass them! I remember running barefoot all over the mountainside, using slingshots that we made to shoot mouse birds, hanging around my brothers to get in on/compete in everything they did, playing in the furrows, and catching frogs. Many of these things we did with the Carlson, Aano, Smith, and Johnson kids. Life was an adventure, and there was little to stop us in our exploration—no threats or things that could harm us, just expansive freedom and infinite possibilities.

Carlson and Simonson kids on the back steps of our red brick house – left to right Kay, Roderick, Becky with Sandra behind, Nathan with Jonathan Carlson behind, David, and Steve

Being around Mom, I was able to see a lot of medical work, much of it at our back door or on our dining room table. I've helped whenever I could, and this has given me a sense that I could deal with many medical situations and even be innovative in using what is on hand to temporarily "fix" things. After all, didn't the old Maasai herder use a safety pin to hold together his grandson's jugular until help could be found (my mom). Don't worry, I am not setting up a medical practice!!

Anyway, from all this you can see that I have been blessed with a unique and wonderful childhood!

When all five children were home on leave or vacation, we would do campouts. One of Dave's close friends, a Maasai, invited us to his area, which was ideal—a brook, shade, and game all around. On one campout we were surrounded by lions at night. Naomi was sleeping at the edge of the tent, with her head against the outer wall. She woke because her head was being rolled side-to-side, and she quickly admonished her brothers. When she looked around and saw everyone asleep, she discovered that it was one lion that kept batting her head with its paw, presumably because it looked like a ball. She moved away from the edge of the tent and went back to sleep. None of us were aware of this because she did not make a fuss about it, but the lions did not give us much sleep either that night. The stories were great the next morning!

Remembrance

In recent years, many church groups have come to experience and learn about God's work in Tanzania. People from high school age to the elderly, have been sent by their churches and colleges. We have enjoyed being included in many of these visits. One group was not able to make the journey from southern Tanzania but sent questions by email. There were many questions about our "call," others regarding the present day role of missionaries. One question was personal: What was the hardest experience in your life? This had me searching my memory. The experience that came first to mind is this.

Our third term was in the remote and beautiful hills of northern Tanzania, at Loliondo. We were quickly adjusting to this new assignment and the housing given us. The family found the place exciting, and we were happy. Our connections with the "outside world" were dependent on the mail delivery, which Bhaqwan Singh brought from the post office in Arusha. He made the trip once or twice a month, to restock his *duka* (shop) and collect the post, so when the private bag arrived, it was just like Christmas. (A year later we had radio contact with Arusha.)

We had been in Loliondo about three months when one of the mail deliveries had been three weeks coming. There was great eagerness to sort out the stack of letters. I saw four brown envelopes that I recognized as telegrams. A feeling of fear griped me because this was so unusual. I carefully took them and left Dave to sort the rest. Going into the bedroom, I closed the door and arranged the four, according to the dates sent.

Opening the first, I read my brother's message: "Mother has had a major stroke, and we wonder if you can come home."

With shaking hands, I read the second: "No word from you. Mother has had a second stroke and is critical. Are you coming?"

At this point, I knew what the two remaining would say: "Mother died last night. We have received no word from you. Can you come for the funeral?"

The last informed me that they had taken mother to her home church, in Barron, Wisconsin, where she was buried. "Dad having a very hard time." There was great concern by my non-response. Little did they know of our lack of communications.

Even when we know that death will come for all of us, there is that heart-wrenching pain when a loved one is taken. As I wept, Dave comforted me, and the young African pastor and his wife who were staying with us enveloped me in their sympathy. Our children had gone to boarding school, so only our three-year-old Jonathan was home.

As weeping released much of the pain, God replaced it with many reminders of his love. The Catholics have a station/church in Loliondo and a hospital in Wasso, which was five miles away. The news reached them, and a delegation of three Austrian sisters came to offer their sympathy. It was my first meeting with Mother Amadea, an older woman whose love radiated from her wrinkled face. Sister Guida was a bubbly, younger woman, and Sister Alma was a gentle, soft-spoken woman. They told me that a Mass had been offered for my mother. I thanked them

Dr Watchinger, Sister Alma, and Sister Amadea

for this gift of love and comfort. I assured them of my mother's deep faith in her Lord and Savior. At this, the young Guida said, "Oh, she was a Catholic!" I assured her that we were all God's children.

An interesting postscript to this first meeting came four years later, after many wonderful times together. We went to the hospital often, sometimes to visit parishioners who were hospitalized, sometimes to assist in surgery, and at visits of the Flying Doctors. We would always have chai (tea) with the sisters and the doctor, Father Watchinger. As we prayed together, a special bond was formed. When we left Loliondo, they had a farewell for us and, as Sister Amadea tearfully hugged me, she whispered, "When I get to heaven, I am going to ask the Father to keep a place for you, right next to me."

In the weeks of healing, after the death of Mother, I had the happy memory of our last week of furlough, before coming to Loliondo. Furloughs are always filled with speaking, meetings, and visiting, leaving very little time to be with family. We were told by the mission board that tickets had been issued, and we were to vacate the mission house and come to Minneapolis. Alas, when we arrived with all our baggage and little ones, our passports could not be found. With no place to go, we decided to visit our families. I took the three youngest and went to Wisconsin to be with my parents, and Dave took the two older ones to be with his parents in Willmar, Minnesota.

We had a wonderful week before the misplaced passports were found. My parents were preparing to move to Florida, to be close to my brother, Harold, and his family. Mother was so grateful for my help as we sorted and packed. It was a truly blessed

gift, being together with our families. The children were delighted to have grandparent time and I to have a special mother-daughter time.

Memories of mother

Father

The death of my mother during the first couple of months of our new life in Loliondo was painful. Had it not been for all the love of family and friends, this would have been a long recovery. God reminded me of all the blessings, and I healed. I made the comment, "I pray Dad will be OK." I was so thankful he was near my brother, living in the retirement apartment.

Dad had always been so enabled by my mother, and he missed her deeply. There were several widows living in this complex who were very attracted to my dad, and he received a lot of attention. One, named Amy, became very dear to him, and they were married. I had such mixed feelings about this: How could Dad forget Mother so quickly (only a few months after her death)?? Yet, his loneliness was eased. I prayed for acceptance of Amy and joy for Dad.

Near the end of our four-year term in Loliondo, my brother, Harold, wrote that Dad was showing signs of poor health. He had a weak heart and had episodes of confusion. I said to Dave, "Perhaps Dad will be gone too." My dear husband said, "You will go see him, as soon as I can find money for a ticket"—not just me, but the two younger children, Becky and Jon, too. When Dave decided on things, they are done quickly, and within weeks, we were on our way to Florida.

Harold met us in Orlando and brought us to his home, in Winter Haven. His wife, Marlene, and two sons, Paul and Mark, welcomed us warmly. After settling and unpacking, we drove to the retirement center to see Dad. It is difficult to explain the feelings I experienced, seeing Dad without Mother. Then we met Amy, who was so unlike Mother. I had feelings of loss, some betrayal, and yet such joy at being with Dad again.

The week that followed was precious, as Dad came alone to Harold's home, and we sat together on the lovely lakeside ad-joining their house. I had never experi-enced this closeness to him; he was always so busy with his congregations when I was a child. Now, some eighteen years after going to Africa, we sat to-gether and he shared stories of his life which I had never heard. Most of his life, he had kept a journal and had written many beautiful poems. He shared some with me.

Dad

Becky and Jonathan were having a wonderful time with this grandpa. He also was pleased to have this time with them. Cousin Paul was working at Disneyland, and we spent a glorious day with him there. They enjoyed getting to know their uncle, aunt, and cousins.

With only a week left to stay in the States, we said goodbye to our precious family and flew to Minnesota to be with Grandpa and Grandma Simonson. We had been there just two days, when

I received a call from Harold. He could hardly speak, so Marlene told me, "Dad died." He had a ruptured aorta and had died instantly.

What can be said? God had given me such a great father, whom I had just begun to know and love, even more than as a child. We had shared so much in this last gift of time. At his funeral and burial in the cemetery next to Mother in Barron, Wisconsin, there was victory and thanksgiving.

CHAPTER SEVEN

Two Continents and in Between

Furloughs

Our first furlough, after five years, was perhaps the most exciting. We would be reunited with family—bringing along four grandchildren, we had left America with only two. Our parents were delighted. Only after having grandchildren of our own, did I realize how precious they are and how often our parents must have missed them. Both sets of parents were still very active in their work, but they came to visit us whenever they could.

We were given a house, owned by the church (American Lutheran Church) in Moorhead, Minnesota. Concordia College,

Nathan, Naomi, Stephen, Dave, me, Rebecca 1960

our alma mater, was only four blocks away and we enjoyed being welcomed back by many schoolmates and faculty. The choir concerts gave me the greatest joy.

That year, 1959 through 1960, was filled with many events. We were invited to speak in many churches; Dave traveled most of the time. We had the eventful trip to the World Series in Chicago, at the invitation of Walter O'Malley, owner of the Dodgers baseball team. There was the Maasai study time in Florida with Ruth Shaffer. Some of these I have mentioned elsewhere.

Goodbyes are never easy, but we were very eager to return to Tanganyika and all we had come to love there.

The second furlough, 1964 through 1965, after another four years, was equally exciting. With five children, very little money, but with invitations from several friends, we decided to do a "grand tour" of Europe. Packing as lightly as possible, we were on our way.

Greece

We flew to Greece first and were treated royally by the Paeros family (a rugby buddy's family). The wonders of this land,

Front – Rebecca, me Dave and Jonathan. Back – Nathan, Naomi, and Steve 1964

with ancient buildings and history, were appreciated by all, even three-year-old Jonathan. We walked around the Acropolis and the Parthenon, which were beautiful; the view over Athens was amazing!

Italy

Our next stop was Italy. My interest in art was renewed by reading the book, *The Agony and the Ecstasy: Michelangelo*. We located an inexpensive hotel, bought freshly baked bread and bottles of water, organized the kids, and were on our way.

Rome. St Peter's, the Sistine Chapel (I was mesmerized by the ceiling), the catacombs, and the Coliseum (where we envisioned the great agony of early Christians being devoured by lions) were special sites. For the three older kids, this was a learning time they still remember.

Venice. We again found a hostel, loaded the bread and water into backpacks, and walked the sidewalks along the canals. One funny incident occurred when we found ourselves in a group of American tourists. As we walked together, Jonathan was behind an obese woman, whose generous backside was just at his eye level. Maybe the bouncing tempted him, and he reached out and pinched her butt. She spun around, thinking some lascivious Italian man had done this and, to her surprise, it was our three year old who gave her his impish smile and said, "Hi, lady" (pronounced Yadee). She swept him up in her arms and kissed him.

Rebecca, me, Naomi, Steve, Jonathan, and Nathan in the Coliseum in Rome

Florence. This was the city I insisted on seeing, as so many great works of Michelangelo are found there. We fol-

Naomi, Steve, Dave, Jonathan with water bottle, Nathan and Rebecca sitting on the curb waiting for me. Florence

lowed the same routine. I should assure you we did not live on just bread and water, but splurged on fruit and one good spaghetti meal each day. The day in Florence was my day, and the family trooped along, to the hill where the magnificent statue of David stands. I was spellbound (probably an embarrassment to the family). Then we went to the famous doors. By the time we reached the Uffizi, where I had hoped to see the main paintings, the family was tired. Steve said, "Mom, you love Michelangelo more than us!" Dave decided, "Enough! We will sit here on this bench and wait." When I returned, an hour later, I found them sleeping, domino fashion, on the bench, and tourists were taking photos of them!

Germany

Next we traveled to Germany, where we had been invited to stay with dear Pastor Patzig and his daughter. Steve and Naomi remembered "Grandpa Pepsi" from the time he stayed with us at Ilboru.

We took a train, saving us a night's lodging as well as providing views of many beautiful parts of Europe during the daylight hours. We received a warm welcome, when we reached Munich and were taken to Schwabuck. One afternoon we were invited for afternoon tea to the home of a grand lady, Frau Meister. We were informed of her great support for mission work in Tanganyika and that she was a very wealthy lady. We dressed up in our best clothes, gave the kids threats of punishment if they disobeyed or were unruly, and went with Patzig to this impressive home to meet this lady. What a tea party we had! A long table was covered with white linen tablecloth, china, crystal, and cakes like we had never seen before—layers of chocolate, cream, and berries. Dave and I were in awe, not only of the abundance but also of how perfectly our kids behaved. Frau Meister was also impressed: "I had been told that American children were very naughty, and now I see these children have great manners." To reward this good behavior, she gave them each a silver spoon and excused them from the table. She had a maid take them to her garden where cherry trees were abounding with the best cherries we had ever eaten. (There are no cherries in Africa). This was a highlight. They did not even have tummy aches from this time in the cherry trees!

Norway

My father had kept in touch with several relatives in Norway and suggested, to them and us that we should take time to explore our roots there. Dave didn't have addresses of his relatives but remembered so many places of which he had heard.

I had the naive idea that perhaps my relatives would be poor (like those who came to America) and probably not understand English. What a surprise when this tall, handsome man drove up in his Mercedes and greeted us in perfect English! My second cousin, Od Olson, owned one of the leading delicatessens in Oslo. We then went on to meet another, a beautiful woman who lived with her husband (who owned the Viking Hotel, one of the big hotels in Oslo); she had been a flight attendant with SAS. Her flawless English and gorgeous home was far from "poor."

We were then taken to yet another relative who lived on and owned much of Holmenkollen, the famous ski jump area. Their home was very old but beautiful. When we came into the living room, I recognized a large painting on one wall—an original by the Norwegian artist, Monk. This home had been taken by the Nazis and was their headquarters during the World War II occupation. In the largest command room he showed us the threshold that had been worn deeply by boots, where soldiers entered and did their "Heil Hitler." The threshold was kept "as is," to remember that period in time.

We were experiencing so many new things and were in awe. Why did my grandfather ever leave Norway?? That could be another book.

After a delicious smörgåsbord lunch at a chateau on Holmenkollen, we thanked these amazing relatives whose names I no longer remember. Olson, a name that fills many pages in the Oslo directory, could be one of them.

An interesting story was told of my grandmother, Maria. She was one of the thousands of Olsons and decided to legally change her name to Nordby. After doing that, she married an Olson! When they immigrated to America, she convinced Grandfather to take the name Nordby. So I was a Nordby who is probably related to many Olsons.

From Oslo, we moved on to Stavanger, to be with the Aano family who had been with us at Ilboru. Their hospitality matched the way we had been welcomed everywhere. A boat trip up the fjord was very beautiful. We were interviewed by the Stavanger newspaper and felt a responsive interest in Africa and our work.

The Norwegian hospitality continued on the ocean liner, Oslofjord. We boarded in Christianson. We were given a fine cabin, well suited to our enjoyment and comfort. There were many activities for the children, which gave Dave and me time to relax and enjoy our friends, Verce and Marcia Fuglestad, who were also returning from their work at Bumbuli in the Usambara Mountains in Tanzania, and Bill and Lynn Smith. All together we were six adults and fifteen children. The big treat for all of us were the smörgåsbord lunches. There were huge blocks of Gjetost, a very special goat cheese, which was a pure delight. (A special knife was available so we could take as much as we wanted.) We did have some wild weather on the first day which delighted Steve (and the other kids) but left most of the passengers seasick!

Our furloughs were always filled with a variety of experiences and opportunities. The second furlough was spent in a mission house in Northfield, Minnesota, at 10 Lincoln Lane. I will always remember the warmth of our welcome there. Women from Bethel congregation had stocked our fridge and cupboards with freshly-baked bread (by Mary Nystuen) and other needed food from many women who have become lifelong friends.

On our first week of settling in, two friends from our school days came to welcome us to worship at Bethel. Pastor Arvin Halvorson was a classmate of mine from Oak Grove; his wife, Twila, was a North Dakota friend from Concordia. This just added to our thankfulness at being in Northfield. Several other classmates from Concordia welcomed us at the first service. Mity (Miles) and Myrna Johnson had been close friends; Mity played football with Dave, and Myrna and I were in a play together at Concordia. Mity was the director of the St. Olaf Band and Myrna was running the Northfield Arts Guild where they produced theatrical plays.

On our way back to the States for our third furlough, we made a similar trek through Europe as we had earlier, and we again took an ocean liner from Norway to the U.S. Dave had been putting money aside to buy a car in Germany. He went to the VW factory and bought a kombi, a minibus that made the rest of our tour so much easier. Traveling on the autobahn, riding on a ferry, laughing at German exit signs (*Ausfarts*) provided all sorts of new experiences. We drove up through Denmark and took the ferry to Norway.

On docking in New York, we retrieved our VW van that we had purchased in Germany and used in Europe and drove to Loudonville, New York, for a couple days with our Shaffer "connection." Some of Roy and Betty's children were in college, Marilyn was starting high school, and Roy was studying as well. We had a memorable night at Saratoga at an outdoor concert of The Fifth Dimension. We then drove from New York to Minnesota.

The two Europe trips are so mixed together in my memory that I cannot seem to separate many things we did. We did visit England on the first trip to Europe, but I do not recall whether it was on the way to the U.S. or on the way back. We did visit Gwen Hiskins, the English nurse who had helped deliver Jonathan in Arusha. Naomi's memory of this trip was going to Trafalgar Square where hundred of pigeons were flying about, being feed by people; some flew into her hair and pooped on her.

We also visited Dave's brother, James, and his family in Ethiopia, where he was a missionary doctor. It was a memorable trip in the things we were able to see and do with Jim and Shirley; we visited the excavated church of Lalabela where some of the first Christians worshiped and had wild rides packed into their LandRover as Jim manouvered his way on the hairpin turns on the narrow moun-tain roads where there was nothing but air on one side. Ugh!

One memorable event happened during this furlough. During our second term in Tanzania, Dave spent time with Crossroads Africa, two groups that came to work on various projects. We became close friends,

Jonathan and Rebecca with me amongst Ethiopian people

as they often came to our house. Side note: They will always remember Naomi, because we asked her to say grace at one of the meals with the group. She stood up and in a loud voice said, "Rub-a-dub-dub. Thanks for the grub. Yeah, God. Amen." We do not know where she learned that!.

During our third furlough, Dave received an urgent request from the director of Crossroads Africa: Would he be willing to come to Toronto, Ontario to give the address for their fund-raising gathering. The speaker who was to have given this address was Martin Luther King Jr. He had been put in custody and would not be able to come. What an honor to fill in for such a wonderful man! "We will fly you and your wife here." Again, my parents agreed to come stay with our children. What a great occasion! Dave needed to rent a tuxedo which barely fit him, and I don't remember what I wore. The banquet was held in Toronto's finest hotel, with hundreds of guests. We marched in with the director, governor, mayor, and other dignitaries, and were seated at the head table on a stage facing the guests. The first course was brought in and I looked at the guests, who all seemed to be staring at me! A moment of panic struck as I wondered what was wrong with me. The gentleman on my left whispered, "They are waiting for you to take the first bite." I lifted my fork and smiled at the gathering; with smiles all around, the feast began. Dave's speech was great and received a standing ovation. The following morning we were given a tour, which included Niagara Falls.

Perhaps the most memorable part of our third furlough (back to 10 Lincoln Lane) for me was going back to work at the Northfield City Hospital. The children were old enough to handle their own care, so I worked four nights a week. At this time, the dress code had been relaxed, so I did not need to locate my old cap or "whites." I found this very strange at first and could find nothing in the casual dress (slacks and loose tops) to indicate what position each held. This quickly changed, as I became acquainted with the loving and fun night crew. A long-time attachment devel-

Grandpa Edward and Grandma Olga staying with us in Northfield

oped with this group, and until this day, forty years later, Diane Boyum (the head nurse) remains a close friend. I made myself memorable one evening when I agreed to fill in briefly for Diane in the ICU. There was only one patient, an elderly man on life support. Monitors and such had not been available in my student days or in my simple clinics in Tanzania. I was shown how to read the heart monitor and told that all should be fine, as the patient was resting. They went off to their meeting, and I sat bedside by this dear man. He woke and stretched his arms above his head and let out a huge gasp. I looked down at the monitor and saw only a flat line. I looked out in the hall and asked the night aid to summon Diane. Without even checking his pulse, I took his hands in mine and began praying the Lord's Prayer. As Diane and others rushed in, the old man opened his eyes, smiled at me, and said, "That is the nicest thing anyone has ever done for me." Relief, mixed with deep embarrassment, swept through me, and the story of this passed through the staff (and town). What actually had happened was that in stretching the man had accidentally pulled off the heart monitors. "When in doubt, pray."

Our children fit into the Northfield scene very well, and friends they made on these two furloughs in Northfield, through church and school, became a fun part of their lives. Trips out to the Nystuen farm were always a delight. Barb Nystuen (Glasgow) was in fourth and ninth grades with Naomi, then came out to Tanzania for Naomi's high school graduation in Kenya; they also traveled through Europe together. Their first year at Concordia, they were roommates, and they are still best friends today. Mary became my "sister," and we are still that to this day. The boys loved riding with "Uncle" Paul. One day Nathan, as we came to

Mary Nystuen with me

Barb (Nystuen) Glasgow and Naomi 2008

visit, sighed and said, "Home on the barn," a phrase we all adopted for each visit.

On our third furlough, we went to Holden Village, a beautiful retreat center in the Cascade Mountains of Washington State. Being with many from places all over America and being enriched by the teachings of gifted speakers was truly restorative. Just Dave and I went on these retreats and found the time together walking and meditating so very meaningful. The greatest blessing of our weeks there came one night, after evening vespers. There was a canteen that sold treats, among my favorites, ice cream. Standing in line with us was a woman of great presence and interest, Jean Wahlstrom. The conversation began with the choice of ice cream; we both were anticipating the same kind. The conversation quickly moved to who, what, and where. She was a Minnesotan from Braham. Did she know the congregation and family Bonander? She did, and then we began sharing about our call to Tanganyika. I shared the story of my "first call" at the age of fifteen years when meeting Richard Reuch, at the wedding of my uncle John to Ruth Bonander.

Jean was a teacher at the Lutheran Bible Institute (LBI) in Washington. This "God incident" became a "connection" of great blessing for us and now Tanzania. We invited her to come see. She and her friend, Cheryl, came to visit the following year. They caught what I have come to call "Tanzanitis"; the only cure comes with becoming a part of this great land and its people.

Jean had met and married Marv Kanonen, an intelligent, lovable Finn. At this time, Dave had complete enough of the Maasai Girls Lutheran Secondary School (MGLSS). These amazing people were called by the ELCA, and they came and gave life to so many. Jean, with her many gifts, became teacher, pastor, music director, confidant, and inspiration. Marv, with his many gifts, became a teacher of English at both MGLSS and Moringe Sokoini, another Lutheran secondary school nearby. His other great gift was his work with Alcoholics Anonymous (AA), a much needed program. His endeavors have given hope and healing to hundreds in Tanzania. He is a writer of novels and crossword puzzles (a favorite pastime of mine). We thank God for these special people!

The next furlough, we were given a three-bedroom apartment at the mission apartments in St. Paul, right next to Luther

Seminary. We quickly found some missionary friends who were back on furlough from several mission fields. Great! The couple managing the apartments became another "connection," Ruth and Dan Vaagnes. Ruth is the sister of our daughter-in-law, Annette.

The mission board had agreed that I would attend the University of Minnesota, to take a nurse practitioner course. Unfortunately, the university had canceled that program, so I began classes in public health. I was told by the registrar at Concordia College that I only needed one credit to complete my B.A., so I enrolled in a course in botany as well as the health classes. I loved being back in the academic world, even though I

My graduation from Concordia College Moorhead, Minnesota, 1983

felt like a mom to all my classmates. Concordia encouraged me to attend their graduation. Many of my former classmates were now teachers and administrators at Concordia, so as I received my B.A., there was an extra hearty handshake. Such fun! Dave found it amazing to be married to a 1983 grad. Both Dave and I, separately, have been honored by Concordia as distinguished alumni.

Our terms on the field were shortened, and furloughs were only three months. The children were entering college, and we were kept very busy visiting

Simonson brothers and wives at an OBA gathering. Luther & Audrey, Jim & Shirley, Bonnie & Paul, me & Dave.

congregations on speaking tours. Dave's continuing involvement in Operation Bootstrap Africa gave the annual gathering such deep value. Dear friends who had faithfully supported this program gathered, and it was a "family" reunion of great encouragement and thanksgiving.

O'Malley

Dave's work in South Maasailand resulted in some extraordinary "connections." This area was a hunter's playground. The abundance of game drew many hunting expeditions, many of them led by men known as "white hunters." They would bring clients from all over the world and set up campsites, from which they would hunt. Dave came to know some of these men and was always welcomed in for a meal or chai.

On one such occasion he was introduced to clients from America. Walter O'Malley was a name Dave knew; he was the owner of the, then, Brooklyn Dodgers baseball team. He and several executives wanted the "big five"—lion, leopard, elephant, buffalo, and rhino. The "white hunter" from Kenya was not well acquainted with the area and had not been very successful in locating these animals. After Walter had spoken with Dave and learned that Dave was familiar with this area, he asked his hunter if he might ask Dave for help. The hunter was very thankful, and because Dave had a few days available he agreed to take just Walter. It was a great time of bonding and the beginning of a strong friendship. Dave was able to help Walter complete his wishes for the "big five."

After the group returned to Arusha, Walter threw a big dinner party for the group and us. He asked if there was anything I would like. At that time, one of the missionaries was leaving and wanted to sell his piano. I had hoped we could buy it, but the asking price was more than we could pay. Dave told Walter about this, and the piano was mine! The rest of the story was like a fairy tale.

We were on our first furlough, living in a mission house in Moorhead, Minnesota, a year after Dave's meeting with O'Malley. The Dodgers had made it to the World Series against the Chicago White Sox. Dave was on deputation, and my parents were staying with me. Dave decided to send O'Malley a tele-gram wishing him well in the series. I received the reply tele-gram: "Dave, you and your piano-playing wife must come imme-diately to Chicago." I called Dave and then the airline to buy tickets. My parents were there to care for the children, so all seemed right that we go. Dave came home; we packed our bags, picked up our tickets (paid fully by O'Malley), and were on our way.

This would be the deciding game of the World Series, and we arrived in Chicago after the game had started, without tickets or even knowing how to get to the stadium. Dave was able to call before we took off into all these unknowns. Walter just asked our flight number and said to leave the rest to him.

As we were landing in Chicago, the announcement came that "Dr. and Mrs. Simonson, please be prepared to disembark immediately on landing." Little did we know what was ahead of us! We were met, as soon as the plane was stopped, by the chief of police of Chicago. He welcomed us like royalty and put us into a taxi. With a police escort of three motorcycles, we sped through Chicago (sometimes on one-way streets going the wrong way). The taxi driver said, "This is the first time in my life I've ever had the police in front of me."

When we arrived at the stadium, we were welcomed by more police and three of the other men who had been on that hunting safari. We were whisked off to the box seats at first base and seated with celebrities—Gene Autry, for one. We could not believe what O'Malley had done or what stories he must have told people about Dave. We seemed to be in a dream.

The Dodgers won that game and the World Series! What excitement ensued, and we were caught up in it. We learned later that Dave's brothers were watching the game on TV and as O'Malley was being interviewed by the press, where he ex-pressed his joy and congratulated his team. Then, he excused himself, as he said, "My friend from Africa is here, and I want to welcome him." Dave's brothers told us their amazement at hearing this.

We were welcomed so warmly and invited to join O'Malley and all the "big wigs" involved with the Dodgers, to ride with them to the hotel. We stopped by a Catholic cathedral where they all went in to offer God thanks for the victory. The driver said to us, "That's the richest church in Chicago today."

Things continued to feel like a dream—a beautiful suite next to O'Malley's, meeting so many fascinating people, listening to the safari buddies telling stories of their hunting, all this after winning the World Series.

My joy came from meeting Mrs. O'Malley. She was such a quiet, unassuming woman who had recently undergone treatment for cancer of the larynx. She managed to speak in a whisper through a tracheotomy tube. I expressed my wonderment at being included in this occasion. We were to go to a celebration dinner, and I felt I would be inappropriately dressed, as I only had my simple black suit. She assured me that this would be OK; she then wore a black suit as well, to help me feel that I fit in. What a kind and generous woman!

The celebration was another eye opener for me. All the players and wives were honored. Each woman was given an orchid corsage which had been flown in from Hawaii. The glitter and opulence was beyond description—certainly a world I had never witnessed before. I felt a deep sense of not belonging. Coming from a country of great need, I experienced a moment of judgment at all the expense. The table of hors d'oeuvres was adorned with ice statuary and loaded with so much food it could have fed our Tanganyikans for a month.

After a night in Chicago, we returned to our normal, down-to-earth lives. We were thankful for this one night of a fairy tale.

Work and Pleasure

Medical

My hopes and dreams of using my medical skills were realized in many ways—not in the major schemes of saving lives (though there were a few), but in many minor roles.

The first term seemed to be completely focused on raising children. I often had opportunity to treat others for minor problems and, on occasion, to deal with emergency cases. As I worked with women in Bible study, sewing, or just visiting, I would teach health issues. Many times, lessons on prevention—proper diet, cleanliness, and such—were welcomed. It was

Caring for Maasai mother and baby at my backdoor

always an honor to be asked about personal health problems, as our trust in each other could be developed. One such case was a thirteen-year-old girl who came for treatment. She had been circumcised and was bleeding, to the point of collapse. These cases would not be shared without trust and, after dealing with her situation, there became a special bond, a "connection."

Our children were the normal, active ones, with lots of cuts and bruises, but only a few occasions of real concern. The one episode that did give me a scare came when one day I could not find our two-year-old Jonathan. He had gone into the guest room and found a package of anti-malarial pills, all nicely wrapped in cellophane. He was happily unwrapping and eating them. I took him immediately into the hospital; he was already becoming quite ill. Thank God, the British doctor had just come into the emergency room and was able to pump out all the pills. The dosage he had eaten would have killed him.

Through the years there were many areas of medical need that were open to me. The first organized commitment was a decision to begin maternal/ child health clinics in some of our church dispensaries. The government was promoting these clinics and made supplies of vaccines and other medicines available. The first of these clinics was in connection with Selian Hospital. There was an out-patient building and a maternity unit.

Nurse Paulina standing between me and a visitor at Selian Hospital

One doctor, a nurse, and a midwife cared for the patients, and one day each week we held the maternal/ child health clinics clinic. Word of this clinic spread quickly, and our attendance numbers rose. We were primarily working with well babies and pregnant women. A trained mid-wife handled the deliveries, so our role was with the babies. These precious, beautiful babies became a part of my joy. We were given charts for each child by the government, on which we could record growth, weight, as well as vaccines given. Should there be a health problem, a referral was given and noted.

Several friends joined me, and we became a team. We also began other clinics. One of the more lasting "connections" came one day, when a shy fifteen-year-old girl came to the clinic. She was neither pregnant nor with a baby. She came looking for an opportunity to learn and to help. Paulina was a quick learner and an enthusiastic helper. We came to depend on her in many ways. Now, after forty years, she heads a hospice program under the Selian church program, in what is now a 100-bed hospital. She cares for over a thousand terminal patients, through teaching their caregivers the methods and love needed. Her example of Christian love has touched so many lives and given hope and comfort to thousands. I can only thank God for sending this precious soul to us.

One funny episode, we team members remember, concerned a determined chicken. Our sterile supplies—it was my job to take home and sterilize all needles, syringes, and other equipment—were laid out on the delivery room table, and vaccinations were done in that room. We kept chasing this chicken away from the room, but she was determined. She flew in through a window and very happily, delivered her egg on top of our sterile field!

An exciting opportunity was offered to me during our second term. Would I be willing to work with the Flying Doctor program, under the auspices of African Medical and Research Foundation? This organization was begun by Dr. Michael Wood and was based in Nairobi. They had expanded their program to include Tanzania and had placed a plane here, to bring medical help to the less-reachable areas. This would be a volunteer position, on a stand-by schedule, that suited mine. I was thrilled to be a part of this. I loved flying and seeing these people and places.

Dr. Harold Housman was the pilot and doctor with whom I took most of the flights. He was gifted in both positions, although at times he was a bit too daring in his piloting of the six-seat Cessna. The airstrips were often tricky, and the weather conditions, often unpredictable. Harold enjoyed catching thermals as we took off toward escarpments. One very fun part of our flights together came after Harold had taught me to do some basic flying. After our clinics were finished and we were airborne, he would turn the controls over to me, while he recorded the procedures done at clinics. What a treat to have that control! One day, as we were returning to Arusha, I flew too close to a military training program. A flare was shot at the plane (it missed); we both expected some trouble with the government. Thank God, there was none.

Some of our clinics were in small dispensaries, while others were under the acacia trees. My work was primarily well baby care, much like our maternal/ child health clinics clinics. If dressing or injections were required, those were my responsibilities. When the doctor felt the patient should be hospitalized, we would bring them to the nearest hospital with an airstrip. This connection with Flying Doctors continued in many ways in the years to come.

During our years in Loliondo, I was often asked to handle some of the clinics in their program. There was a good airstrip near the Catholic hospital in Wasso, where Dr. Wood and other surgeons made monthly visits to treat the patients in need of their expertise. Having had surgical nurses' training, I was often asked to assist. There usually was an anesthetist who came with the surgeons, but when he decided to leave, I was asked: Would I be willing to take a short course in anesthesia, using an ether/oxygen machine. This was one part of surgery to which I had always said, "Never". Now, I was offered a chance to learn this skill. Never say never! Two intense weeks in Nairobi followed with a great anesthesiologist in the hospitals; I learned how to intubate, regulate, and control the ether/oxygen machine.

Dr. Watchinger and me on Flying Doctor clinic trip treating Maasai under an acacia tree.

The day I was to do an entire surgery anesthesia is one that I will never forget. I was taken to a makeshift hospital where procedures were done on polio victims. There had been an epidemic of polio some years before which had left many with useless legs. My case was a sweet young man who was to have both legs amputated and to receive prosthesis later. He was slightly sedated when he came into the theater, but he gave me a smile as I told him that God was with us, and he would one day walk again. I followed all the procedures—injections, intubation, and had him nicely breathing in the mask. The hours that followed were difficult as the legs were being sawed off. The smell and sound were nauseating. I foolishly kept my face too close to the ether machine and *nearly* passed out. Again, God restored me and all was good. The supervising doctor praised my work and pronounced me ready to do the job on my own back in Wasso Hospital.

During the anesthesia crash course. I was lovingly cared for by Roy and Betty Shaffer, who had moved to Nairobi. Roy was also a part of African Medical and Research Foundation and Flying Doctors.

These years, as an anesthetist, were to bring a few dramatic episodes. The first happened shortly after I returned from my training in Nairobi. One evening Dr. Watchinger called to say there was an emergency in Wasso. A young Maasai warrior had been brought in with an acute appendix which needed immediate surgery. He would do the surgery, although he confessed he had not done such a surgery since his years in medical school. This would be my first solo, too. I drove the five miles to Wasso and set up the machine. One of the sisters scrubbed with the doctor. I successfully anesthetized the man, and surgery began. I noticed the doctor had opened

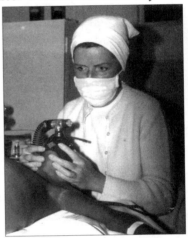

Me as the anesthetist during an operation at Wasso Hospital

several medical books, which he had set up along the window sill. I had my books open as well. This had to be one of the longest appendectomies ever performed. I was given a sterile glove and assisted in retracting and cutting out a highly inflamed, foot-long appendix. Amazing! I was so concerned that the anesthetic was sufficient, that it took the warrior a whole day to wake up. But he did wake up, and he survived!

At another time, a runner arrived at our door, asking me to come immediately as his young brother was seriously injured while herding cows with his grandfather. The boy had a short spear and as he was sticking it into the ground, the spear handle hit a rock, bounced up, and cut a major vessel in his neck. I took the old LandRover and raced for several miles over open grazing land with the runner beside me, directing each turn. The boy looked almost lifeless as his grandfather brought him to the car. The child was covered in his own blood. The grandfather had taken a big safety pin, found the vessel, and pinned it together. The trip back to Loliondo and then to Wasso seemed endless. Praying and driving like a rodeo rider, we finally found the doctor. I knew where all the needed supplies were kept. The child was saved.

One of my favorite stories (and there were many), happened one day as I was working with the surgeon, Mike Wood. We had done several cases in the morning and the last of the day, was a "biggie."

A frail Maasai elder was to have an immense hydadid cyst removed from his liver. The surgery was going well when I noticed that his blood pressure was dropping. Dr. Wood was very concerned, as he could not find where all the blood was coming from. We had no blood supply, so unless he could find the "bleeder," the man was lost. At just that time, Dave was stopping by the hospital to greet us and looked through the observation window. I saw him and cried, "Get Dave in here! He's a universal donor!" Dave was put on a gurney next to the old man, and a direct blood transfusion took place. The doctor stopped the bleeding, and the old man survived. A weakened Dave joined in the moment of prayer and thanksgiving. In the days of recovery, the shriveled old man would raise his skinny arms and proclaim, "I am a *simba (lion)*! I have the blood of the pastor!"

Another medical area, for which I was not especially trained was midwifery. In nursing school, obstetrics was part of the nursing program that I enjoyed, but I never had been given the opportunity to deliver a baby. That changed in Tanganyika, as people came to me in labor, to be taken to the hospital. Several cases were unusual. For the strong of heart and the interested, I have recorded them below.

A woman came saying that they needed me right away, and there was no time to take the woman to the hospital. Naomi wanted to come with me to help. I grabbed whatever I felt was needed—scissors, towels, clamps, etc.—and we went running to a hut about a quarter of a mile away. Night had fallen—it does quickly near the equator—and as we stooped to enter the hut, there was almost total darkness. A small fire burned with water boiling. This gave the only light. The woman was in the final stage of delivery, so I received the child, clamped and cut the cord, cleared the mucus from the baby, and all was well. I was thankful and proud that the delivery went well.

Then, the placenta should come. We waited. I massaged the tummy and prayed. I knew nothing about how to deal with a retained placenta. Out of the darkness, a very old woman approached, and in her hand she held the belt a woman uses after circumcision. Was she going to use that beaded, dirty belt to bring out the placenta? I was scared, but when I was told that this was the traditional midwife, I stepped back. To my utter amazement, she rammed the belt into the woman's mouth. The retching this caused had an instant effect, and the placenta was out. I am sure the medical world would gasp. I did.

One evening I was asked to take a mama to the hospital to deliver her child. We had been given a lovely Volvo sedan, so I had good transport. This time, I took no equipment as I was assured that the mama "wasn't that far along." The road to this *boma* began as a proper road, became a trail, and my Volvo and I were soon wedged between thorn bushes. The woman was brought to the car. No sooner had she made it into the back seat of the car that she cried, "It's coming!" Women ran to get blankets, a razor blade, and string. All went well, but my backside was firmly attached to thorn bushes. By the time the placenta was delivered, the baby bundled into blankets, and my backside released from the thorns, all were rejoicing and praising God. I felt mother and baby should be checked out in town, but they laughingly said that there was no need. Mama and baby were escorted home.

The next morning, I was amazed to see the father with the baby at my door. My heart sank, and I feared something dreadful had happened. The father's smile eased that fear, as he handed the baby to me, "He is yours." That, of course, gave me a start. The father went on to explain that this child would be told the story of his birth and my part in it. He then proudly announced, "His name is Volvo!

Theater

One of the many gifts I have received from my dear grand-children, as well as from our children, has been their involvement in theater. As they perform with great talent, my theatrical bones quiver with pride. Of our children, Naomi has played major roles in many plays, including musicals; Steve has had major roles in two musicals (wife, Marilyn, has acted and helped with many productions); and Nate has had a minor role in a play (wife, Susan, has done costuming for very many of the plays). Ten of fifteen grandchildren who grew up in the Arusha area and attended the international school have participated in numerous plays, some major roles

Even as a young child, I was acting, not just "acting up." God gave me an over-active imagination and the urge to pretend. This sometimes got me into trouble, when reality and imagination clashed. Yet I continued to participate and enjoy a good theater or school performance. Both in high school at Oak Grove in Fargo, North Dakota, and at Concordia College, Moorhead, Minnesota, I found excitement in performing in theater productions. After marriage, working, motherhood, and coming to Africa, my theatrical opportunities took a different path. As a mother, I still enjoyed making up stories for the children, with many animated sounds and gestures, but there was always a longing to be involved in theater.

Arusha was very much an English government center in the 1950s, and the British love theater, so they built a place for enthusiastic local expatriates to perform. The Little Theater was designed solely for the purpose of stage productions. It was a small building in the center of the Arusha business area. There were no flashy marquees or notice boards to announce which play was being performed, but word always circulated through the community regarding our latest project. A single side door opened into a lobby with a small bar. There was seating for approximately 200 patrons in the main theater, with the chairs on elevated tiers, facing the stage, that was about twenty feet by twenty feet. There was more than adequate space on each side and at the back of the stage to accommodate scene changes. At the back of the building were three dressing rooms, toilets, and utility space for costumes and stage props. It was well planned but quite crowded when the play had a large cast. A lighting/

projection area was located over the lobby and was well equipped for the size of the stage.

A dear artist friend, Di Bannister, had invited me to paint with her. One afternoon, as we painted together, she began talking about an upcoming play, the traditional English panto-

Artist at work

mime, for the Christmas season. My interest prompted me to ask if anyone could audition, and she enthusiastically invited me to come. This was the beginning of several fun years at the Little Theater, and it could not have happened at a better time for me. Our children were all in boarding school, we had recently moved into our new home, Dave continued to be involved with the vast area of his ministry, and I had time I could spare to be involved. What an opportunity! By this time, the early 1970s, there were many Americans, with various aid programs, located in Arusha, and they also became involved. Over the years, the cast had gone from a predominately British cast to an international cast, including Tanzanians.

English pantomime is unique in many ways. It is not mime, as we Americans know it. A well-known children's fairytale is often used as the basic storyline, written to include local events and people. The audience's participation, in booing at the villain and cheering the hero, is very important, and it allows everyone to get into the act. If the story involves a prince, the prince is played by a woman. When we did Cinderella, the two ugly stepsisters were played by men.

My first role in an English pantomime was the good fairy who cared for the animals (played by children), in an expanded version of "Snow White." As a matter of fact, the story line was so expanded that there was very little of the traditional fairytale to be found. A wicked witch had goofed when dealing with the

Me, furtherest right, in Music Man.

Hello Dolly! Matchmaker.

seven dwarfs. As she was casting her spell, using Swahili, she confused the numbers, which resulted in fourteen dwarfs. What a fun way to become involved with the theater! Together with all the stagehands, we numbered around thirty-five people from at least six different countries. It was the beginning of a truly international time in Arusha theater.

While I was serving as a nurse for Americans working on a road-building program in Tanzania, Joann Ramsay, the wife of the USAID director, Bill Ramsay, became a very close friend. She had amazing musical gifts and took on the direction and production of "The Music Man." By this time, Americans had nearly taken over the Little Theater. Very gifted musicians were found in both the Baptist and Lutheran communities, as well as from the growing numbers of expatriate non-governmental organizations (NGOs). The sets, choreography, and backstage crew brought the number of those involved to nearly fifty. The logistics of the production were a challenge, but the end result was great! I was cast as Eulalie Mackenchnie Shinn, which gave me an opportunity to sing, dance, and be a comedian. I loved it!

In the following years it was great fun being involved in many plays. If I were to choose my favorite roles, it would be the part of Dolly in "Matchmaker" and Martha Brewster, one of two old maids who poisoned old men, in "Arsenic and Old Lace."

These roles allowed me to expand my talents, to go beyond my mother, missionary, and nursing persona.

An ironic, full circle experience was when the play, "Night of January 16th" by Ayn Rand, was put on in Arusha, just before the Little Theater closed. At Concordia I played the lead character in that play. In Arusha I played the part of an old Swedish cleaning woman, a witness against the leading character.

My Direction Connection

One day in 1980, a lovely Ugandan woman named Grace Akello greeted me after church and asked if I might read a play that she had written. As we became better acquainted and as she became more comfortable with our friendship, she shared some of the background and inspiration that drove her to write this play. It often led me to tears.

She and her family had narrowly escaped many atrocities under Idi Amin. The horrors she described, were greater than any family should have to endure, and yet this family, never doubted God or their faith. Always God was given full credit and praise for their miraculous deliverance. Grace's play, "He Touched Me," reflected Gods mercy in providing their salvation and described other aspects of her life in Christ. These were depicted in a series of episodes from the Gospel, where the loving and healing hand of Christ had restored and delivered. As I read the play, I felt God's inspiration and a desire to see it performed by members of the newly-organized English-speaking, interdenominational congregation who were, at that time, worshiping in the beautiful Anglican church, Christ Church. Grace was delighted and, together with the vicar, Chris Scott, we began to raise interest in the production. Several were already active members of the Little Theater and were keen to get involved. It was decided that it would be performed as part of our Holy Week activities.

Casting was a joy. God provided the perfect person for each and every role. Rehearsals became a spiritual experience. We always began our time with prayer, and we felt ourselves being drawn into an intimate closeness as we enacted the profound stories under God's guidance. We were again supported by so many willing hands that sewed the costumes, provided lighting, and performed music. We performed this play in the sanctuary of Christ Church. It did not require sets or many props. The sanctuary was a fitting place, surrounded by stain glass windows depicting scenes of the life of Christ. The play was received warmly, and the message of Christ's healing and loving touch became a blessing to both the audience and performers. He touched us!

"Would you be willing to direct?" The year was 1985, and several of the regular Little Theatre directors were either on furlough or committed to participating in some other role or project. Well, the show must go on!

Feeling very inadequate, yet wanting the theater to continue, I agreed to give it a try. "The Wizard of Oz" was chosen by the members. It was a difficult musical with a large cast. I felt it would indeed take a wizard to pull it off, and while "wizard" was not on my resume, with the amazing help of everyone, we put on a grand show.

The greatest challenge was the music. Our piano was a quality instrument, but we had no one to play the complex score. I then remembered Linda Jacobson, a fantastic pianist, whom I recently had met in Nairobi where she and her husband, Dr. Mark Jacobson, were living before coming to Arusha. Missionaries have no problems asking others for help! I felt no embarrassment in calling her and asking if she would be willing to record a rehearsal tape for us and then travel to Arusha and accompany the live performances. Being the energetic woman she is, she agreed, then prepared and sent a tape that we used for all our rehearsals. Our daughter, Naomi, and I also played the piano, as needed, but the use of the tape worked surprisingly well and provided the musical continuity that was much appreciated by the performers.

Our cast was terrific, truly an international ensemble. The Lion was played by a Scot, the Strawman and Tinman were played by Dutchmen, Dorothy was a small American woman who looked about fourteen years old, The Wicked Witch of the West was our Naomi. It was fun directing Naomi in her first stage appearance, and she was so good. There were several kids in the first rows who wet their pants when she came on stage shrieking and cackling!

Years later, in the early 1990s, the Arusha Community Church, which had met at the Anglican Church, now had its own building. The congregation had grown with people that had moved to Arusha from many countries. There were many talented members, with enthusiastic ideas of ways to enrich participation. "Let's do a play! How about 'Godspell'?" Never having seen the play or movie, I was not sure if I could direct it, but my friend, Mary Ender, a gifted music teacher working at the International School, said she would do the music if I took on the direction. We ordered the script and found that the original play ended with Christ on the cross rather than with his resurrection. Mary and I felt that no one would mind if we wrote our own ending, providing the glorious "He is risen" message that is the very foundation of our church. We did not think about copyright laws or licensing infringements.

During auditions, one of many God-directed things happened that confirmed we were following his will. The church announcement each Sunday urged people who wanted to be a part of this play to come for an audition. The number of those wishing to have speaking or singing roles exactly matched the number of roles in the play, and each casting was perfect! Mary organized a children's chorus and a five-piece band, with herself on the piano. To my delight, Steve, Marilyn, and Naomi were part of the cast. Again, the essential part of each rehearsal was beginning with a word of prayer. A feeling very similar to *déjà vu* came over me as we became bound together in purpose and joy, as we had done in "He Touched Me." Our daughter-in-law, Susan, is a genius at getting everything one needs at *mitumba*, our local second-hand goods and supply store, and she handled costuming. Every talent and every need was filled by someone from our Arusha Community Churh family, including sound, lighting, and programs. It was indeed a labor of love for all of us. We gave two performances at our church, after which we were invited to Moshi to perform at the International School. I felt we had really arrived when we were asked to take the show on the road.

My Movie Connection

Our children attended Rift Valley Academy in Kijabe, Kenya, when they reached high school age, beginning during our years in Loliondo, in northern Tanzania. We would make several trips a year to visit them, and while there we would usually stay at the Mennonite Guest House in Nairobi. On one such visit, Ken Anderson and his Christian production company were producing a film. We became friends, and Ken asked if I would care to watch them shoot a segment of the movie being filmed in the garden.

At dinner, Dave and I talked of our work among the Maasai in Tanzania. Ken was very interested and told us he was working on a script for a movie he hoped to produce about the Maasai. He had met several Christian Maasai and was inspired by their commitment to their faith. He asked me if I had ever been in a movie or if I had ever been interested in theater. As we talked and I shared my limited involvement in theater, he asked me to consider being in the movie that they planned to film the following year. It sounded exciting, and I agreed. Because it was all in the formative stage, he asked for my address and said he would contact me when things were ready.

A year went by without any word from Ken, so I felt it was nothing more than a good intention. We went to visit our children and again stayed at the Mennonite Guest House. Who should be there but Ken Anderson! He was excited to see me and told me it was an answer to prayer. He had lost my address and name, but felt I was the one for the role of the mother of an eight-year-old boy in his completed script. He had his complete cast there and was ready to start filming the next week. Would I consider staying to take this role? Dave encouraged me to stay, "It might be fun having a movie star for a wife. (The "star" part was rather a stretch.)

When Ken gave me the script, I was quite amazed at both the story line and the fact that there were only basic directions. The story had an exciting twist. An American family was coming to Kenya, where the husband would be researching an existing program in which elands were domesticated. The family was to live at the Hopcraft Ranch, which is located some twenty miles from Nairobi, on the Athi River. The Hopcrafts, had a pet cheetah that was to be a major part of the story.

The twist in the story comes when the boy, Bobby, becomes very fond of the cheetah, Tonka, and meets a Maasai boy of his own age. Together, they share many exciting experiences, but one adventure angers some Maasai warriors and they kill Tonka, causing a split in the friendship of the two boys.

The Maasai family consisted of strong Christians who were very sorry for these events and asked Bobby's family to attend their church. The family had little time for church but felt they should do their part to provide reconciliation. At the service, surrounding by loving Maasai and God's love, the parents are touched by this love and together ask Christ into their lives. A visit to the *boma* afterward confirmed again that Christ would be central in their lives. The final affirmation came with Bobby's friend giving him a baby cheetah.

Ken arranged to have all the scenes in which I appeared, shot in the first week. Our first location was the Hopcraft Ranch, a unique house and setting. We arrived in several cars, with all the equipment. I was still in the car gathering my things when a huge and magnificent cheetah leapt from the nearby bushes, jumped through the open front door of the car, and began licking my face. Eyeball to eyeball, it was love at first sight.

Ken left a lot to our interpretation of his directions. Some lines that were key to the scene were learned on the spot. He gave us enough direction about what he wanted and left the rest to us. It was amazing how well that worked, and there were very few re-takes. The entire cast was made up of local people with little acting experience, but with Ken's direction and God's blessing *Wild Country*, a fine movie, was made. The experience was great.

Some interesting post scripts: Our daughter, Becky, and I were invited to visit her roommate's parents in Zambia. As we walked down the streets of Lusaka, several people asked me for my autograph. We were told that *Wild Country* had been shown on TV as well as in several churches in the area. That was a first for me. The film was also used by several of the missionaries in Tanzania as a way of reaching the Maasai. The response was good. To God be the glory!

Writing Academy

On three of our furloughs, I had the privilege and joy of attending the Writing Academy, a Christian group dedicated to encouraging and supporting writers. My "sister," Chris Hefte, was with the founding group organized by Dr. Harley A. Swiggum, author of the Bethel Bible Series, in 1978. She knew of my love of reading and writing and felt this would be the right group for me. She was so right!

Every year, these writers would gather for an intense week of encouragement with established writers. The three times I was privileged to attend, the group met at the Mount Olivet Conference and Retreat Center, a place of beauty and peace located

Writing Academy retreat – I am the fifth person from front left in white dress and white hair

near Northfield, Minnesota. Our times of worship, the camaraderie, and the gift of committed Christian writers has been one of God's great connections and inspiration. Another great "connection" was with one of the retreat speakers, Walter Wangerin. We had met him previously, when he came to Tanzania as the speaker for our missionary retreat, and we became friends. We had also visited his home on a trip to Indiana and took a cruise up to Alaska with him. What a truly remarkable man!

Dave and me on an Alaska cruise with friend Walt Wangerin

In the next chapter, "Table Blessed" and "Five Circles of Love" are from my time at the academy. Other short stories and prose are in the Appendix, "Fruits of the Writing Academy."

CHAPTER NINE

Move to the Hill

A Table Blessed

I am a table! For over thirty years, the one comment I have heard over and over from those sitting in chairs around me is: "If only this table could talk!"

My first life was in a forest of the high woodlands, in northern Tanganyika (now Tanzania). Those of my immediate family were very rare (*Fagaropsis angolensis*). We basked and grew tall in the fertile soil, until it was decided by hu-

Table in the dining room.

mans that this fertile land could be better used for growing crops. We were all cut down and our roots pulled from the rich soil. What would become of us? Many people came to take our branches for firewood; others came to select what would make good timber for building; and, sadly, they took the rest for a huge bonfire.

A young missionary, living at the edge of our forest had pleaded for our preservation. He admired our strength and beauty, so was deeply saddened when we were cut down. He was also a man of vision and ambition who, when his attempts to save us failed, selected the best of our various families and bought us for future use in his many building projects. We became churches, schools, and health clinics.

When he and his family were relocated to a mountain, 200 miles away, my closest family members became a part of their unique home. The master designed it as five intertwining circles, reflecting the round mud huts of the African people the family serves.

Our wood is golden green, with lovely swirls and lines, perfect for me, the dining room table the master carefully crafted. But I am not special because of my beauty or strength, but because of how I am used.

I sit in a place of wonder; light pours over me through tall windows, framing the awesome beauty of Mt. Meru. This location would be pleasure enough for some, but for me the greatest joy comes from the great experiences I observe.

I have witnessed the joys and sorrows in the lives of the family who made me. My once smooth finish bears the marks of teething babies, dents pounded by protesting children, long scratches from toy race cars, and indentations from letters written. There are light rings from the countless cups of hot coffee or chai and casseroles that are set upon me. I am the center for daily meals as well as banquets, receptions, and teas. I seat twelve comfortably, but often fourteen or even sixteen are squeezed in.

Each Easter, over 100 people gather for a sunrise worship service, followed by a potluck breakfast buffet. On other holidays, my family gathers to celebrate. Christ is the center of this home, and his presence is always invited, whether one person sits quietly or a hundred gather. How I love to hear the children, as they join hands, with all the family, sing, "Oh, the Lord's been good to me. . . ."

Most mornings, after the breakfast dishes are cleared, the Mama of the house begins her Back-Door Clinic. The most heartwarming moments are when a thick, warm blanket is placed on me, to receive a newborn child or an ailing infant. As they sleep or wiggle about, they are lovingly examined, treated, bathed, clothed, and prayed for.

There are times of deep sadness as well, my finish wet with tears, as family or friends, reveal news of suffering or death. There are tears of repentance, together with confession and forgiveness. The Lord's Supper is shared—the first when I was newly made and the youngest son, together with six others, was confirmed and received his first communion, surrounded by family and friends.

Many important decisions are made by church leaders who rest their elbows on me as they pray and struggle with the needs and concerns for the expansion of God's Kingdom. Blueprints have been spread on my wide surface, to enlighten not only the builders but also the many guests who wish to help make them realities.

Memories are made here. People from many lands and every color have graced this home,from bishops to beggars, ambassadors to back-packers. All alike seek nourishment for mind, body, and soul.

Tables are usually associated with food, and I am no exception, but the number of other activities I have hosted are uncountable. Children find me the best place to paint, put together puzzles, assemble Legos, and celebrate birthdays. Grownups like to lean on me while they absorb the beauty outside and ponder deep thoughts. Many letters have been written, photos sorted, books reviewed, and accounts filed on my welcoming surface.

I have stood in this one room almost my entire life and have no desire to be moved. Where else could I better serve or be surrounded by such love and laughter? The prayers, a part of each gathering, are answered according to God's gracious will. Even I, as a table, am blessed.

I wrote the story, "Table Blessed," years before this story. I was later encouraged by several writers to expand and write a story about the whole house, using the approach from the viewpoint of the house.

Five Circles of Love

I am the house in which the "Table Blessed" sits in my spacious dining room. Like the table, I have often heard, "What stories these walls could tell!" Before telling these stories—there are so many—I must relate some history, which is related by the mama of the house, to the countless visitors who come.

This spacious hilltop was given to the *Bwana* of the house by the Maasai/ Arusha people when he was made an elder in their tribe. This beautiful foothill of Mt. Meru has the vantage point that offers views of Meru as well as Arusha City, which stretches below. For this is a gift of love and respect the family is forever thankful.

When deciding just what style I should be, the *bwana* wanted me to be as African as possible, with all the comfort and openness needed. When the family was on furlough, they shared their ideas and dreams with an architect friend, Bob Quanbeck. As ideas were shared, a concept of five circles emerged—each to be intertwined and with its own function. They sat at a dinner table and began drawing circles by tracing cups, salad plates, and dinner plates. So began the idea and when the family returned a blueprint of the footings was done. From these, the structured plans remained solely in the head of the *Bwana*.

Near the entrance to their property, they built a small sixteen foot by sixteen foot house, in which they lived the five

Front view of our house

years it took to build me. Everyone's active lives left limited time for the construction.

Those five years, were a story in itself. To house a family of seven was a challenge too, yet I heard these were rich and fun years. A loft with a retractable ladder was used for sleeping space for the five children. They were all in boarding school, so only on vacations were they home. There was an "outhouse" and an attached stall for a

On the porch of our 16' x 16' house.

shower. Water was brought in and used sparingly. Much of the cooking was done on a two-burner kerosene hotplate or on a BBQ pit built outside. A small kerosene fridge kept food safe. No electricity. A store house was added and a section of that served as an office. Even as I was being built, great efforts were being made to establish terraces on the hillside, rock retaining walls were built, and trees were planted as well as gardens of bananas and vegetables. These multiple tasks were done by many; the children were learning building skills as they worked with their father and two Tanzanian builders, Marko and Godbless.

There was one story I heard told often that was both amusing and descriptive of that period. Friends from America had come and were staying at the lodge nearby. Lenore, a dear friend of Mama, wanted to spend the days with her. The five kids were nearing the time to return to school, so Mama was busy sewing name tags into their clothing, washing clothes, and making things ready. As Lenore and Mama were visiting, a sudden rain began, so half-dried clothes were brought inside and hung on hastily strung wires. Then *Bwana* came and said he had invited the Bishop for supper. A hasty menu was planned, but the rice needed to have the rocks and insects removed. Would Lenore help do this while other foods were located and prepared? She had never known one could eat rice like this but agreed. Sitting amid the dripping clothes, she cleaned the rice as best she could and later joined in the dinner of rice, BBQ meat, vegetables, and fruit shared with the bishop on the veranda. These kinds of occasions seemed to happen often in this household.

Meanwhile, I was being built, as directions were given. Marko and Godbless had worked with *Bwana* on many churches and school projects and were very aware of his exactness on everything. One day, as they were rebuilding a round wall, Marko said, "He has spent years teaching us to make things level and square; now we must build in circles!"

The bedroom section was built first, because they heard that the parents of *Bwana* were coming. This circle included three pie-shaped bedrooms, a toilet/bathroom, and a toilet/shower for the master bedroom. A center circle gave access to all four rooms. This was a "dinner plate" sized circle, with proper ceilings and space over it to be used for storage (as the children left for college, their "stuff" filled these upper rooms).

At the other end of this house were built two "tea cup" size circles; the farthest circle was the office for *Bwana*. Next to it was the official front entrance, with an unusual floor of cross-cuts of a wild olive tree, set in terrazzo. A beautiful arched door with brass knobs (spikes) came from the island of Zanzibar, and was said to prevent elephants from breaking in.

The last two "dinner plate" sized circles, were the final and

Front door with spikes to ward off elephants

Front entrance with crosscuts of wild-olive in floor

perhaps, the most challenging. I am very difficult to explain, because I am so unique. Circles, each interconnected to each other, signify "wholeness" and "completeness." I have the dining room, which holds "the table" and a complete curved wall of windows with the full view of Mt. Meru. Over the dining area, a full circle creates a loft, which also covers the kitchen and part of the living room. It resembles a spoked wheel, with beautiful red cedar beams attached to a center pole.

The biggest and highest circle was the last to be built, and it incorporated several African concepts: a fireplace in the center, open and round, with a poured cement hood and a chimney that reaches the thirty-foot peak of the roof.

Many family and friends have gathered around the fireplace in the cold season. A half-circle rock wall separates the area around the fireplace from the kitchen. Concrete sitting benches, covered with cushions, line the wall. Open areas on the top of this wall have wooden pillars that help support the loft above. Many open spaces between these pillars are perfect for displaying the many art objects, mostly ebony Makonde sculptures. Half of the area surrounding the fireplace, that has the wall and benches, is three feet lower than the living room floor and is called "the pit" by the grandchildren. It is a cozy place where they played games, read books, and just relaxed. The living room itself has a grand view of Arusha, through a half circle of windows. Many of the "stories" have taken place here.

Each "circle" has its own pitched thatch roof. The thatch is made by people along the coast from the palm tree branches into shingles. These were then lined with plastic, creating a waterproof as well as a protective covering.

Have I confused you enough with my self-description? You really must see it, to better understand. Some of the delightful comments I have heard are: "This is one of the most unique houses I've ever seen." Or, to the Mama, from a woman architect, "You have a very romantic husband." On the free-standing stairs to the loft, a German architect, "You are forty years ahead of our architects." By a spiritual woman, "This

Central fireplace with rock wall of the 'pit' – taken from the living room

house reflects God's love and wholeness." These words are cherished. I am not grand but rather a reflection of the lives of those who built me.

I was ready for habitation in 1972, even though many things were still in progress—"the Table," some cupboards, and other furnishings. The stories began.

My doors are open most of the day - welcoming all who come. One day, as Mama was baking in the kitchen, she heard the voices of several German-speaking people. She went to the front door and greeted them. They were wandering around admiring me. Upon being welcomed, they ordered coffee and settled themselves around "the Table." Mama had chocolate cake, so with the coffee, she served them this. They were so interested in me and wondered if I was just a restaurant or also provided lodging. One said, "You must enjoy working in such a beautiful place." At this, Mama couldn't resist telling them that this was her home. The embarrassment was replaced by laughter, as Mama told them that they were very welcome and offered them more coffee.

Among the hundreds of memorable visitors who were invited into my five circles, were three Maasai women. The *Bwana* had brought them in from a *boma* far from Arusha. Never had they seen a city or a *mzungu* (white person) home. Even though I am "traditional African" in many ways, I was a far cry from their "traditional" Maasai home. The Bwana was bringing them in for some medical attention and wanted Mama to check

them out first. As she welcomed them into the house, there were exclamations of both fear and wonder. Slowly the Mama explained through interpretation from Swahili to Maa what each room was used for.

Living room.

Above the living room entrance was hung the Maasai shield of the *Bwana*. It bore the special star that indicated he had killed his lion. This brought great responses of admiration and discussion. On the coffee table Mama had placed a life-size clay sculpture of a Maasai warrior's head. Screams of horror split the air as they approached this. The Mama lifted it off the table and tried to explain that this was made of clay as they bravely touched the eyes and stuck their fingers up the nostrils to be sure. Whatever were their thoughts? Did missionaries take heads off and cover them with clay?

They had never seen a stairway or steps but wanted to climb up into my loft. This they did on hands and knees with squeals of laughter. The young boys of the house often wore sandals made by the Maasai, and a pair was left beside one of the beds. One Mama found them and excitely showed them to the other two. Where was the warrior? Under the beds? Behind a screen? Did they belong to the head on the living room table? So many questions were so difficult for Mama to answer.

After crawling down the stairs, Mama took them to the bathroom. One had never seen a mirror and as she passed the sink with a mirror above, she spied this face looking back at her. She greeted "her" and saw the woman speaking at the same time. Where was she? Was there another woman behind the sink? She stuck out her tongue out at "her" and shrieked as the other woman did the same. Mama was trying so hard not to laugh but stood with her and explained that "we" were looking at ourselves.

As this drama went on, another of the ladies was standing in the toilet, washing her feet and finding that delightful. The tub in this bathroom is sunk below floor level. The third woman had climbed into that and felt it could be a great place to lie down in. She liked it so well she asked if when they returned some day to stay with us, she could sleep there.

They were very reluctant to leave, even though they maybe still had grave doubts about the fate of the Maasai warrior and the lady behind the bathroom mirror.

Another "walk-in" experience that was very unusual also occurred because of my location and attraction.

A young man presented himself at my door (didn't just walk in like the Germans) and explained why he had come. His accent was new to the Mama and as she invited him in, he clarified that by saying he was Russian. He went on to explain that he was walking along the road below and was fascinated by my appearance. He felt drawn to come learn more about me and those who lived within. He was welcomed in, and Mama called the *Bwana* to come meet this young man who said his name was Nicholas. There was a strong interest/curiosity on the part of these two men in each other, so coffee was offered and served at the "the Table".

The question was asked, "What brings you here?" This was of interest to all three present. The *Bwana* answered by telling Nicholas that they had been called by God to bring the Gospel to the Maasai. Nicholas's response: "So you are missionaries; I am an atheist." This opened into a lively discussion—Christianity vs.

Atheism, Capitalism vs. Communism. The two men were enjoying this discussion and when Nicholas looked at his watch, he quickly excused himself but asked if he might return. He was welcomed to come any time, the *Bwana* saying he was often gone on his work but coffee was always available. So began these almost furtive visits, to spend time in conversation with the *Bwana*. He said he needed to be careful about coming but never explained why or who he worked for. There was an air of mystery about him as well as an air of familiarity; he was always welcome and suddenly disappeared without a word.

Twenty-five years later, the *Bwana* was sitting in his big chair on the veranda (an addition made to me for times just like this). The *Bwana* was semi-invalid following a major stroke; the veranda became his place to be a part of all activity around him. A taxi drove up, and a middle-aged man jumped out and ran to the *Bwana*, with arms outstretched: "I have waited twenty-five years to come see you again. I am Nicholas!" He went on to say that a day didn't pass without his remembering those times shared with the *Bwana* and Mama.

There were tears in every eye as they embraced. "You deserve an explanation from me; you never insisted on knowing why I was in Tanzania." He went on to explain that he was with the KGB, on a secret mission from Russia. He shared that he now was married and had two children. The big joy came as he reached under the shirt and pulled out a crucifix. "You were right, my friend, and Jesus has become my Lord!"

Mama loves to entertain, not just on the stage, but in my space that is open to all. Some of the parties for birthdays, holidays, and weddings are memorable.

Let me describe some New Year's Eve parties: These were done for many years and included most of the mission family and friends. Mama would decide on a theme, and attire was chosen from that: fancy dress, original hats, and sports clothes. One memorable hat was made by the *Bwana*—a toilet seat, a head made of a plastic ball, with a

Margaret 'Mugsie' Friberg and me – very stylish women!

mask attached and two rubber gloves, filled with water and draped over the seat.

Guests would come at 6:00 p.m., be given "bitings" and drinks. Then Mama would start the games. Her favorite was charades. The groups were chosen by playing the mix-match game first; names of famous couples Mama had written on cards (Anthony/Cleopatra, Tarzan/Jane...) she pinned to the back of each (male on male, etc.). They could ask only one question per person, until each knew who they were and who would be their partner for the game. A color code divided them into teams, and the game was on.

At eleven, a light refreshment was served, after which all would move out to the front lawn for a service of scripture reading, sharing of thanks for the past year, and seeking God's guidance for the New Year. At midnight, the church bells all over the city and mountain would usher in yet another year of grace. The scene was almost magical and the love expressed always set a goal and renewed each one.

Perhaps the most memorable gatherings held within my walls are the Easter sunrise services, which began a couple of

A view of where Easter sunrise services are held and an Easter sunrise service

years after my completion, in 1972. People were invited to come at 6:00 a.m. and bring some special Easter food to share for breakfast, which would follow the 6:30 service. All had been prepared on Saturday. Every chair was brought into the living room and arranged facing the window, where an altar had been set up. This was done by placing the *Bwana*'s desk top on the big tribal drum that sits by the windows. The bronze cross and candle holders were arranged and, as guests brought flowers, these were arranged on the altar as well. For years, the late Mrs. Saska and Esther Kinsey furnished these beautiful flowers; in later years, Joke Bruinsma (Dutch, pronounced "Yoka") filled all the vases with lilies.

Easter is often the season of the big rains. Many stories have been told of cars needing to be towed up our steep hill. The sons and grandsons always provided towing service, as well as directing the parking and providing umbrellas. The "sunrise" was often veiled by falling rain or mist, but the light of God's presence was always shining.

As the people arrived, with their baskets and sleepy children, the greeting of "He is risen" echoed everywhere, and the response, "He is risen indeed," started the day with life and joy. Baskets of food were distributed on "the Table"; people were ushered into the living room. Many mothers with small children would choose to sit in "the pit," and older children loved to sit upstairs, along the railing in the loft. The service usually began when all were seated, at 6:30 a.m.

For the first twenty years, the *Bwana* would lead and preach. After his stroke, Mama and family filled the role of leader, and guests would give the meditation. Music and prayer were a vital part of each service, with Linda Jacobson as pianist. Solos by Kris Hartwig were very special.

After the table prayer, directions were given on the breakfast service. The women would open, cut, or display all the delicious food, and Mama would have the coffee, chai, and juice set up. A great breakfast would be had by all.

This sunrise service has become a tradition for many and will continue, hopefully for a long time to come. As people left, most went on to their churches for that service.

Happenings

The invitation came from Concordia College in Moorhead, Minnesota: "Could a choir of thirteen girls be selected to come for a two-week concert tour in Minnesota?" People from the States had come to Tanzania to visit the new secondary school for Maasai girls. Some had sponsored a girl, while others were just interested in the exciting school. Concordia College had established an endowment that would bring two graduates from Form Six each year, on full scholarships. They wanted to bring the choir to create interest and secure funding.

Maasai girls with Dave and me at the Maasai Girls Lutheran Secondary School, Monduli

Thirteen girls who had never been further away from their traditional mud and wattle villages than the secondary school were to perform for the people in America. The opportunity was fantastic, and the enormity of preparing such a feat in two months' time seemed unattainable.

Two Tanzanian teachers and I, a retired missionary, were asked to accompany them. Other teachers at the school began the selection from the school's large choir. The choice of songs, the presentation, the choreography, and countless email communications, were handled by Jean Wahlstrom and others. This was an opportunity of a lifetime, a step in faith on the part of the hosts, as well the choir.

The unusual events surrounding our preparation and travel caused many people to comment, "What great luck," and "Amazing coincidences." These words didn't convey how we felt about these special happenings.

The first unexpected evidence of God's care came with the procurement of U.S. visas. The entire group was required to make the twelve-hour bus ride to Tanzania's capital, Dar es Salaam, to be interviewed by an exacting and skeptical immigration officer. Students traveling to the U.S. had become suspect, as many had gone, never to return. We had been warned not to expect an easy time. After the girls had been individually interviewed, the officer needed further convincing. "You are a choir, so please sing for me."

The girls sang with such beauty and vitality that the office workers, guards and other applicants rose to their feet in applause. The officer stated later, "I was transported to cloud nine!" the papers were signed immediately.

After blessings, from our bishop, we boarded the KLM flight from Kilimanjaro to Amsterdam. We had reviewed flying procedures sufficiently, and the nine-hour flight went without incident. Disembarking was something else. The busy Schiphol Airport in Amsterdam was like nothing the girls and teachers could have imagined. Wide-eyed and awed by masses of people moving in every direction, they needed to cling to each other. I left them briefly at the arrival area while I checked out our departure time and gate. Upon my return, I found two young African men talking to the girls. The conversation went something like this:

"Where are you coming from?"

"Tanzania"

"Wow! We are from Kenya. Where in Tanzania?"

"We are students from Monduli."

"No kidding, what school?"

"The Maasai Girls' Lutheran Secondary School."

"You are Maasai?"

"Yes."

At this point, the language switched from English to Maa, the language of all of them. Animation replaced skepticism on the girls' faces. The big surprise came when one of the young men said, "My grandmother had a part in the establishment of that school!" The girls knew his grandmother well, *Koko* (Grandmother), had lovingly cared for them when they came to the school. Of the hundreds passing by, would this happening be just coincidental?

We had two hours before checking into our next flight, so we moved to the shopping area of Schiphol. Greater activity surrounded our group. I needed to leave them again for a few minutes, so they remained close together. I returned to find the teachers and girls in conversation with a distinguished African gentleman. He introduced himself and told us he was a doctor, from one of our Lutheran hospitals in Tanzania. He was on his way to Washington D.C. He could sense the feeling of wonderment and uncertainty in the girls and spoke gently, of all they could experience. His parting words were of encouragement, "Wherever you go in this world, God will be with you."

These two special happenings were in our minds as we made our way to the Meditation Center on the second floor of Schiphol. In the peace and quiet of the lovely chapel, we gathered to read, sing, and pray. As the girls sang, people came in to listen. One woman asked who they were, and then thanked us for adding a blessing to their day. The verse of scripture for the day came from Romans 8:28: "We know that all things work together for good, for those who love God, who are called according to his purpose." We carried these assuring words in our hearts as we returned to our next flight.

Our reception in America was great. The concerts were a success. Everywhere we traveled, we were embraced by loving people. When we returned to Tanzania and shared our memories, those "happenings" in Schiphol, were remembered with great thanksgiving. To meet people of your own race, tribe, and country, halfway around the world, was one of God's greatest surprises.

Good luck? We would say God's love

Coincidence? We would say God-incidents.

CHAPTER TEN

Miracles and Connections

Holy Week

An interesting thing happens as I review my life; so many unusual and meaningful experiences come to mind. Several of these occurred during Holy Week.

Reversing the order of these events from now, as I near 80, they would be: the fracture of my fibula bone on Maundy Thursday 2008, the open heart replacement of Dave's aortic valve and the pacemaker installed at St. Mary Hospital/ Mayo in Holy Week 2004, our airplane crash in 2003 with regaining consciousness on Easter morning, the miraculous intervention of my flight cancellation in 1960 when the plane blew up, and a Good Friday miracle in 1958. This I have not recounted and feel it is very noteworthy.

A Good Friday miracle

In the back yard of our Ilboru home grew a giant wild fig tree. We were told by the older people that this tree was planted by holy women who sought fertility by placing small offerings at the tree base. It was a magnificent tree that gave shade and beauty to our place. We had a workshop on one side and parked our car next to that.

I believe the year was 1958, when the big rains were long and heavy, with the ground saturated to a great depth. Little did we know that the root system of this giant fig was very superficial, but vast.

At 5:00 a.m. on Good Friday morning, I awoke with Dave jumping on top of me and covering me with his body. Then there was a tremendous crash! The house shook, the sound of shattered glass and falling bricks filled the air, followed by complete silence. Groping to find the torch, we sat stunned. What had happened?

We then heard the frightened calls of Naomi and Becky. Help! The girls shared a bed in the room adjacent to the back veranda. Stepping over fallen bricks and other debris, we looked into their room. A great branch of the fig tree stretched inches above the girls. Shattered glass covered them, and we realized the girls were under the blanket. Naomi said that she had suddenly awakened and had pulled the blankets over them without knowing why—God's intervention. A second later, a huge branch came shooting through the window. This was a first of many "Thank you, God" prayers. We told them to just lie quietly, until we could move them.

Steve and Nate were awake in another room, far away from most of the damage. As typical, Steve said as he looked around, "Hey, this is just like a nature walk in our own house."

Their next concern was for their beloved golden cocker spaniel, Sandy; he slept on the veranda, just outside the window that the tree had come through. They continuously called, "Sandy!" Suddenly, out of the wreckage came our dog. He was not harmed but needing lots of loving, which the children lavished on him.

We checked everyone, and no one had a scratch; the prayers of thanksgiving increased. We had no electricity, so we knew there might be live wires (not just the kids), so we gathered the family in the living room that had not been damaged, shared what we knew, that the fig tree had uprooted because of too much rain and had fallen on our house. We decided to wait for morning light before exploring the damage. Praying together, we held each other close.

At daybreak we heard the voices of people coming to church for services—cries of fear as they called our name. Since the tree's branches covered most of the house, they feared we were either killed or badly injured. We came out the front door, which had not been damaged, to the people gathered, amid ululations (high pitched howling sound made with movement of the tongue; women do this at times of celebration) and warm handshakes and hugs.

The children found this fallen tree to be a true jungle gym. They climbed and played, quickly forgetting the fear we all felt as the tree fell. The miracle was that, had it fallen further in any direction, there would or could have been serious results, possibly fatalities.

The first service that Good Friday was a service of thanksgiving!

Our five children each have their own unique stories. After completing high school at Rift Valley Academy in Kijabe, Kenya, the first four went to the States and attended our alma mater, Concordia College in Moorhead, Minnesota. (They didn't know there were other colleges.) Stephen, Naomi, and Rebecca (Becky), graduated from Concordia. Nathan transferred after two years to North Dakota State University in Fargo, North Dakota, to gain a degree in civil engineering. Our youngest, Jonathan, a genius at all things mechanical, chose to go to a technical school in Moorhead for diesel mechanics. They will each share their story later.

Becky

It is Becky's miracle story, I wish to share first. During her years at Concordia, she would find summer jobs. Between her junior and senior years, she was invited to work on a ranch in western North Dakota, and that set the direction of her life. She met and later married one of the rancher's sons, Jim Weinreis. Before accepting his proposal, she had him come to Tanzania, to ask her dad's permission and to meet the Simonson family. We all approved!

Marriage and four children later, they came with the two oldest to visit. It was a wonderful time for all. That was, until one night, when Becky had a grand mal seizure. She had told us of some previous momentary "blackouts," but did not feel they were significant, as they occurred after strenuous exercise. This was big! We held her and watched that she would not bite her tongue, praying all the time. She came around, after twenty agonizing minutes and, as confusion cleared off, she lay exhausted but rational. We called the doctor who gave meds and suggested she be seen by a neurologist as soon as she returned to the States.

They returned home a few days later and, because she was feeling better, she did not go to the neurologist. Naomi kept pushing her to go to a doctor, but it was not until another grand mal seizure that Naomi made the appointments, with the help of Dr. Verce Fuglestad. Becky came immediately to Minneapolis. An

MRI showed a large tumor on the right side of the brain. Further studies, with several specialists, diagnosed it as an astrocytoma. Not only was the tumor large and malignant, but tentacles had reached out to many areas of the brain. The prognosis was serious.

The radiologist set up an appointment for Becky to see her surgeon. Becky and Naomi met with this doctor, and while he went out of the room, they both looked at each other and then each said, "This doesn't feel right." Neither felt comfortable with the surgeon assigned. Just then, the surgeon came back in and said, "If you don't mind, Dr. Yap just came into the office unexpectedly, and he has agreed to take over as your surgeon". God acts in mysterious ways! We learned later that Dr. Yap is a renowned brain surgeon.

I was in Zanzibar when I received word about Becky. I flew back to the States to be with her in Minneapolis, where she was scheduled for surgery, at North Memorial Hospital. This was March 1995.

The night before being admitted, we stayed with our dear friends, Dr. Verce and Marcia Fuglestad. Naomi was working in a travel office in Minneapolis, so she was with us. Several of Jim's family had come as well. We gathered for an anointing and prayer service led by another dear friend, Jim Nestingen. What peace the Lord brought to each of us!

Becky was three months pregnant and the doctors had felt she should abort the pregnancy, but Becky's reply was a strong "No! If God wants this baby and me, we are ready."

We were a large group who accompanied her to the hospital and she was the one reassuring all of us. I will always remember her smile as she hugged and kissed us, before being taken to be prepared for surgery. A wonderful God-incident occurred when one of our Tanzania missionary kids, Mim Monson, came to tell us she would be the surgical nurse on this procedure and assured us that the surgeon was one of the best in the country.

Those waiting hours are the longest I have ever experienced. But we knew that she was not only in the hands of a great surgeon and a nurse we loved, but in God's hands.

Six hours passed and the surgeon, Dr. Yap, came to where we were waiting. With a big smile on his face he said, "You have received a miracle." He explained that all of the invasive tentacles, which several doctors had seen on the MRI, had retracted, and he felt there was no invasion of the rest of the brain. He told us she was still in a serious condition, as he needed to cut the cortex of the motor area of the brain to remove the tumor, and she would probably be paralyzed on her left side. But she would live.

The tears of joy and thanksgiving flowed. Mim Monson came to us and gave further affirmation of the miracle. The staff at North Memorial was wonderful. Once she had recovered enough to leave intensive care, she was put on the rehab floor and I was allowed to stay with her for the several weeks of rehab. Husband Jim needed to return to care for the children. Jim had suffered much and felt torn about leaving but was grateful for my being there.

Those days are so memorable, with many evidences of God's presence. Becky's head was bandaged for the first few days and, when these dressings were removed, she sometimes wore hats or scarves to cover her shaven and stitched head. She was unable to do anything on her own for quite awhile. She told us that when she was regaining consciousness, Grandpa Rudolph (deceased) was standing at the foot of her bed, dressed in his favorite red plaid shirt. He assured her that all would be fine, in God's hands.

One day she started having a temperature, and the stitched area became inflamed. She was taken into surgery, where a four inch by five inch section of skull had to be removed due to an infection. A flap of scalp had been stretched and stitched to cover this pulsating part of her brain. There was only skin between outside forces and her brain. She refused to wear a protective covering, saying all would be OK. This would remain until after the baby's birth, when they would then go in and do repairs.

Her smile was lopsided, but always there for the many visitors. Speech and movement was difficult at first, but with all the various therapies—physio, occupational, and speech—there were daily improvements. It was hard to watch our once vibrant long distance runner and dancer struggle with every movement. Being in superb physical condition and being used to training, she made progress quicker than expected. Each of her therapists showed her so much love, and I felt she was everyone's darling.

She was also checked daily by an obstetrics nurse; all was well with the little one.

When she was not in therapy, she had me wheel her around to visit the many others in rehab, some recovering from strokes, others from accidents, and a few, like Becky, from brain tumors. A very special bond developed among these patients. Becky was always greeted with love, and her prayers were accepted with thanks. It was difficult for her to watch some of these friends die and then wonder why she was spared.

When she was discharged several months later, she was fitted with a brace for her left leg and was able to walk with support. It was time for her to return home and for me to return to Tanzania.

Dave had been lovingly cared for by the family, and I was very thankful to find he had also healed from his surgery, a five-bypass heart surgery during the year past. He felt I should return to be with Becky at the birth, so I again returned at the due date. I had been there only a couple of days and was with her at a therapy session when she went into labor. Only a few hours later, I was allowed to be at the birthing of a beautiful seven pound, three ounce baby boy, whose apgar was 9.9! Another miracle! The doctor said that it was the longest umbilical cord he had ever seen—six feet long—and possibly the many kinks in the cord had helped collect some of the drugs Becky had been given, thereby keeping them from the baby.

Anthony Simon was born at the same hospital, St. Joseph's in Dickinson, North Dakota, where his four siblings had been born, and where I had been born sixty-five years earlier. Becky returned home in two days, and I remained two weeks. I was amazed at her ability to do so much of the care for Anthony with the use of only one arm and hand. She had good help from family and a fine young woman. I could leave knowing she would be well cared for. It is always difficult to say goodbye to those we love so much. Those precious little ones— David (nine), Stephanie (eight), Kristina (four), and Lloyd (one), were thrilled to have the new baby and were a great help to their mama.

A couple months later, Becky returned to North Memorial for reconstructive surgery to her skull. A section of her skull, from the opposite side of her head, with the exact dimensions, was taken and split like an Oreo cookie, and replaced over the open areas of her skull. Amazing! All her follow-up checks have remained free of any more cancer.

An exciting sequel to Becky's story came four years later, when she fulfilled a longtime dream of doing a 200-mile walk, like her dad had done several times for Operation Bootstrap Africa. We began planning and decided to make it a family walk. The route usually walked from Loliondo to Arusha needed to be changed because a gang of Somali bandits had been attacking many on that route. An alternative way was worked out, leaving from Tarangire and walking across much of the area of South Maasailand where Dave had once worked, then east to the Pare Mountains—200 miles of many delights and challenges.

Dave, Steve, Naomi, Nate, Becky, Jon and me - First day of our trek with Becky

Most of the family were a part of this. The youngest, Bethany (three), was carried much of the walk by Susan. Daniel (seven) and Luke (five) did a part. Jonathan provided a back-up lorry, with food, a cook, and tents. Each early morning, after breakfast and devotions, we were on our way. The first twenty miles were really rough for Becky, as we walked through what is called "snare grass." Her left leg and foot, in her brace, were continually catching, and she would fall forward with only her right arm to break the fall. Susan walked with her that first day, and would lift her up and encourage her. Big brother, Steve, assumed this privilege when Susan left after her kids became ill.

At camp I would treat the blisters and bruises. Dave was able to walk the first day, but he also became ill and Naomi took him home. I would walk each morning; after lunch I would climb onto the truck and help set up camp at day's end. The teenagers were always in the lead, loving the experience.

Becky continued with great determination and on the seventh day completed the 200-plus miles. What a show of courage and amazing strength! She did this walk to raise money for a teacher house at the Maasai Girls Secondary School in Monduli.

Fear

I was once asked, "Have you ever known fear from the Maasai people, with whom you live and work?" Perhaps. I didn't answer with this story; it seemed too difficult for me. I had known fear.

In a village near to our home, lived a very influential Maasai elder, an Olaiguianan. He had become a close friend of Dave's and helped him to establish a church in his village. Several of his wives had come to me on various occasions for medical help. We were close.

One day we received an invitation (more like a summons), to come to their *boma* for the celebration of circumcision. Three of his pubescent daughters were to be circumcised that morning and we were to "celebrate" with them that noon.

Maasai woman applies ochre to my neck and face for a ceremony.

Celebrate! My first thought was of a young Maasai girl that had been brought to me, close to death, as a result of blood loss from this traditional custom. All the efforts I had made in teaching and discouraging of this practice at this time seemed fruitless and in vain. I tried to avoid condemnation, but rather approached it as a medical trauma for a woman. I had seen how difficult and sometimes fatal the scarring was to the birth process. Now I was to "celebrate"?

We were welcomed warmly. Dave was taken to the assembled men, who sat under the trees, drinking the native honey beer. Some already quite intoxicated. I was escorted by one of the mothers into the circumcision hut. This large hut was built in the traditional pattern, from woven branches plastered with cow dung and mud. It was larger than the usual loaf-shaped homes, without windows or holes.

As I was led into this total darkness, I was aware of many other women, as they reached out to welcome me. My sight was limited by smoke and the absence of any light. I remained standing and searching for someone I might know. Then the fear began. The hands that welcomed me were soon reaching to stroke me. Drunken laughter erupted from some as they felt me reacting to their touch. The groping and fondling began to be very personal, as hands seemed everywhere. My irrational fear soon turned into desperation, as I felt closed in and trapped by those who were violating me. What came to mind did nothing to quell my fears. I remembered hearing of a well-intentioned missionary woman who had approached the practice of circumcision of young girls with condemnation and anger. The response of many was to circumcise her. She died of shock!

All 'decked out'!

I was in a circumcision hut. Somewhere, there were three young girls who had come through the rite, now lying in recovery. Somewhere was the old woman who had performed this, with a sharpened knife or razor blade. My imagination of what could happen next caused me to cry out to God for deliverance. The women only laughed and continued to explore. Absolute fear gripped me.

Then a soft, gentle, male voice asked me, "Are you afraid?"

"Yes!" I replied.

"Then give me your hand, and I will take you out."

I eagerly extended my hand and it was led by his strong hand. Other hands fell away, and I was led out into the brilliant sunshine. I rubbed my eyes and turned to thank the man. I was all alone.

Plane Crash

"Oh, my God! We're going to crash!" our pilot, Elizabeth, had barely uttered these words when our six-seat Cessna hit the ground, then bounced and cartwheeled, then careened to a shuddering stop.

We were upright, though tilted at a strange angle. As I opened my eyes, I saw Elizabeth struggle to free herself of her harness and drop head-first out of the open space that was once a door. Turning my head, I saw my husband, Dave, helping the three Tanzanians who were flying with us. He kept calling my name and asking if I was okay. The vice-like pain crushing my chest made it impossible to answer, but I nodded at him and smiled, as I noted he still wore his precious black hat. His face

The propeller and nose cone went off to the right, not straight back.

Crumpled wing where fuel was leaking out

was dusted a gray shade from the field in which we had finally stopped—his handsome face, that I loved so much. Someone released my seatbelt, and I was being urged and helped to leave the plane. The door on Dave's side had been torn off as well, so we were not trapped. The urgency to move came from Elizabeth, who was now upright; there was a danger of the full fuel tanks exploding.

Within minutes of the crash, dozens of villagers had come running to the site. They had watched this *ndege* (Swahili word for bird or airplane) flying low over their village, barely missing the trees. Then they heard the crash in their cornfield close by. Elizabeth urged them to move back, from the possible explosion.

We were alive, but looking like death. Dave was feeling pain in his back, yet was able to move about and talk to the villagers. Another Maasai recognized him as the missionary who had helped these people build a chapel and school years before. The elder admonished the people not to loot the plane out of respect for Dave. Looting has become a common practice for a few who find accidents a good picking place. We had crashed a few hundred yards from the highway leading to Nairobi. Someone had found a cell phone and called the Catholic mission we had recently flown over. They were sending cars to pick us up.

A Maasai came to me and put one strong arm around me, with his other hand he took mine to support me. Others were helping Dave, Elizabeth, and the three Tanzanians who appeared not to have been hurt. I felt this man, who gave me such assurance, was an angel. He softly comforted me with words of reassurance, "God is with us. Do not be afraid. All will be well." I struggled to breath, and the pain only worsened. Several people came up to us, laying their hands on us and praying. I tried to apologize for the destruction of some of their crops; they only smiled and assured me that we were of more value than corn and beans.

Dave and Elizabeth had both sustained fractured vertebrae in their backs, the Tanzanians had minor bruises, and my x-ray showed extensive damage to my chest, including a broken sternum with accumulated blood behind it. Dr. Mark Jacobson quickly decided I would require more care than Selian was able to provide. He asked the medical service pilot, Pat Patton (who just happened to have flown in from Loliondo, where we had been heading), to fly me to Nairobi immediately. I was sedated by this time, so I felt very little pain as I bade Dave and Elizabeth goodbye and was taken to the airport.

Mark Jacobson had notified Nairobi Hospital and requested a thoracic surgeon to be on standby. When we arrived, this surgeon was not available, so I asked for Dr. Gikonyo, who had cared for Dave just the week before. The nurse looked at me like I was asking for God! Dr. Gikonyo, I was told, is the president's doctor and held in great regard. They said he was not scheduled to be at the hospital, but they would try to call him. He happened to be in his office writing reports, and he came quickly, bringing the chief thoracic surgeon with him. The care was ordered and prepared—x-rays, EKG, IVs, and countless procedures. I was in the High Dependency Unit, with excellent care, by midnight. It was a long night of constant checks, shots, and observation.

Marilyn and Steve arrived the next day and became my link with Arusha. They assured me of Dave's care and of that of Elizabeth the pilot. Both were wearing back braces and doing well at Selian.

When Naomi, our daughter doing graduate work at the Minnesota State University, Moorhead, was informed of the accident, she was attending a conference in Toronto, Ontario. She booked a ticket, went back to Minnesota to pack, and was on her way to Nairobi.

On Tuesday, after the crash of Saturday, April 12, 2003, I went into a crisis. Every vital sign went berserk—vomiting, no blood pressure, high fever, and erratic, weak pulse. The activity was intense, and I felt death was near. I was so very weak, yet I knew I needed to clear my slate with God. I do not remember being afraid, but rather thankful for all the rich blessings God had bestowed on my life. I asked him to forgive my many sins and to please let me live, because Dave needed me and I would like to watch our beloved grandkids "become." A sense of God's peace and contentment overwhelmed me as I drifted into a coma.

When Naomi arrived on Wednesday she said that while flying she had a terrible feeling that she would not get there in time; this was the same time I was in crisis. Dr. Gikonyo kindly brought Naomi up-to-date on everything that had occurred. He said that he and four other doctors had worked for four hours to stabilize me. Also, that next morning when I gained conscious- ness, a nurse's aide was quietly singing, "Count your many blessings, name them one by one." I did just that. When Naomi first saw me, she said I was the same color as the sheets, so she pulled out some makeup and made me look better. Just seeing her made me feel better! Since Naomi was there to take care of me, Steve and Marilyn headed back to Arusha.

Steve Cunningham, a missionary kid who had grown up with our kids and who is now a pilot, took pictures of our crashed plane and the crash site. Only when we later saw how totally destroyed our plane was were we able to know how God had protected us. The entire engine was ripped off and was thrust off

Tail twisted to back seats

Propeller from the crash is displayed on our back porch as a daily reminder of God's grace.

to the right, rather than the normal direction of straight back into the cockpit. The tail was destroyed, twisted like a cork screw. The right wing folded up into the petrol tank. The doors were gone, torn off. Only the fuselage area that held the six of us was intact. Another miracle was that when the plane first touched down, we were inches away from a deep and wide ravine. The plane bounced, lifted, and landed us just inches from the far edge. At this point, we cartwheeled our way through the corn, into the field, where we came to a full stop.

Two weeks of recovery in Nairobi blurred into a collage of loving care. There were countless attempts to put IVs in my fragile veins, daily dressings to a wound on my arm, and many checks of vital signs. Other patients in the unit seemed to be in far greater need than I. We came to know the families of several and were blessed by the many faith experiences. The name of Jesus the healer was spoken by so many caregivers and staff. One nurse said to me, "God must love you so much, to bring you through all of this!" A missionary friend and his wife brought me communion on the day of my crisis, as well as on Easter Sunday. What a gift!

Passion week has taken on a new dimension for me. As I struggled with the pain and difficulty to breath, I was aware in a deeper way of the unbearable suffering my Lord had experienced as he died for the sins of all humanity. Easter Sunday, with the promise of life, was doubly sweet.

We were told that 100 friends gathered at our house for the traditional Easter sunrise service and breakfast. Daughter-in-law Susan, who had been caring for Dave, led the service, and Dave shared the Easter message, with the crash story. Still unable to stand, he preached from his chair. My heart was with them. The words of this song summarize my feelings exactly:

Because he lives, I can face tomorrow.
Because he lives, all fear is gone.
Because I know who holds the future,
My life is worth the living
Just because he lives!

CHAPTER ELEVEN

Assorted Endings

Wittenberg Award

November 6, 2004

Dave and I have been blessed throughout the years with honors and awards too numerous to mention. Actually, I would rather not mention them, because acclaim and notoriety have never been the driving force behind our mission. The love of Jesus Christ and his Holy Spirit guiding us has been all we have needed.

The years of 2003 and 2004 changed our lives so dramatically, I began to wonder if God was calling us home. The role Dave played was especially altered by all the health issues he had endured. The once physically powerful force, who had built churches and schools and brought so many into God's kingdom, was now reduced to getting around in a wheelchair and relying on others for his most basic care, relying on *me* for most of his care.

All life-changing events require a time to grieve, until acceptance allows one to move forward in a positive way. We were living in our Fergus Falls house while recouperating from the crash. I was struggling through that process, when we received word that Dave and I were to receive the Wittenberg Award in Washington D.C.

The Wittenberg Awards were established in 1990, to recognize Lutheran laity and clergy, from around the world for distinguished service to the church and servant leadership. What a tremendous honor! Yet, would Dave be able to handle the journey? I was still exhausted, physically and mentally, and felt overwhelmed with all that would have to be done in order to attend such an event. Would I be able to handle the strain? After all those years of putting our trust in God, I cannot believe I allowed doubt to enter my mind.

Many of our family and friends arrived in Washington D.C. the night before the awards. Dave's brothers and their wives came, as did my brother, Harold, and Marlene. We celebrated Dave's seventy-fifth birthday in the hotel room together. Naomi and Seth were there, as were friends like Donna Reed from Georgia (first woman to make the Operation Bootstrap Africa walk from Loliondo to Arusha), Pam Erickson Cornelius from Montana, Lonnie Pederson from Concordia College—these three women are Naomi's best friends. Bishop Thomas Laiser came from Tanzania. The Maasai girls who were studying at Concordia College were there. The day of the awards everyone went sightseeing around the city; Herb Morgenthaler had arranged for a special tour of the capital and a meeting with a senator from Minnesota. The National Cathedral was the favorite for many. At the awards, Todd and Betsy Benson (Todd is the son of my first cousin, Stan, and Marie, and is my godson, and Betsy is a daughter of Roy and Betty Shaffer, sister to our daughter-in-law, Marilyn), who lived in Washington D.C. at the time, came. A handsome young man named Dave Simonson, the son of Dave's cousin who we have never met, flew in from California to meet his namesake. There were so many friends that I must apologize for not naming all of them. It was a wonderful time.

The evening of the awards was like a dream. I cannot even recall many of the details. What I can recall, when Jim Klobuchar was introducing us, is looking at Dave with love and adoration through my misty eyes, and seeing him again as my youthful,

Dave and me with Jim Klobuchar.

handsome, and powerfully-driven partner of fifty-three years. How I love that man! Yes, the award was given to both of us, but it was a special gift for Dave at this particular time. His past efforts were acknowledged when he knew he would no longer be able to serve God as in the past.

Jim Klobuchar, our wonderful friend, gave such a lovely introduction that I was embarrassed by the accolades. I was very grateful for his kind words and appreciative of his thoughtful account, of our mission. I would like to include what Jim said in Washington D.C. that evening:

Good evening, Lutherans. Before introducing the Rev. David and Eunice Simonson, I'd like to share a portion of a letter Mark Hanson, the Presiding Bishop of the Evangelical Lutheran Church in America, has written in recognition of their years of service in Africa.

The letter, Dave and Eunice Simonson, is written to you. It reads:

"Before our world became so interconnected by networks of communication and globalized economy, you created bridges between the people of Tanzania and the United States. Your vision of ministry is holistic—proclaiming Jesus, educating all, healing diseases, developing sustainable communities. You have consistently reminded us that we meet the risen Christ, who is the center of our lives, when we stand with those who live on the margins.

"You have invited us to experience the wonder and beauty of God's creation in the Serengeti and in the Tanzanian people. You have extended hospitality to countless visitors, challenging us to listen to the faith and struggles of Tanzanians and to experience our unity with them. You are both modern-day prophets. You have known when to challenge bureaucracy and when to ignore it. You have modeled for all of us what it means to pick up our cross and follow Christ into the world."

I probably don't have to tell you, ladies and gentlemen, that nobody ignores the bureaucracy as eloquently as David Simonson.

This is a night to remember for all of us, hundreds of people coming together with their thanksgiving and their profound respect for those who the Luther Institute is honoring for making this a better world.

And, yet, there are thousands whose faces we can't see here tonight, whose voices we can't hear. But they are here, joined with us in expressing their love and their gratitude for the lives of Dave and Eunice Simonson.

David and Eunice, they ARE here tonight—the Maasai of Loliondo, of Arusha and Kitumbeini, who told you, "You are one of us, forever"; the patients in that little hospital in Wasso; the school children of Tanzania, of Kenya and more; all those thousands to whom, over the years, you made a gift so precious, one they couldn't have imagined just a generation ago—a school, THEIR school.

And those thousands of men and women, Eunice, who with such great affection and complete trust called you "Mama" and still do. And the hundreds of young women from the secondary school for Maasai girls at Monduli— some of them here tonight are college students now. That is a revelation to all of us.

To these, David, you can add the old man whose life you saved, one of many, with your own blood in transfusion.

I'm a child of the newspaper world. The newspaperman meets generals and presidents, kings and quarterbacks. Many of these people are worth their fame. But after awhile they blur into a kind of mosaic of the world's celebrities. But here are Dave and Eunice Simonson. We have seen up close, for many years, their work and mission, their footprints and handprints on the soil of Africa and on the soul of Africa. There is nothing blurred about those prints. They are clear, permanent, and breathtaking.

Six of the Maasai girls who are here tonight are students at Concordia College in Moorhead, Minnesota, where Dave and Eunice studied. And what a beautiful and powerful connection that is to the mission and service of Dave and Eunice Simonson, to the school at Monduli they helped built. That school would have been unthinkable just fifteen years ago in a culture and tradition that have given us so much to admire but which in the past has marginalized women and left them with little hope of dignity. These young women have both today.

David Simonson went to Africa from Minnesota nearly fifty years ago as a Lutheran missionary. His wife, Eunice, was a registered nurse. They arrived in the midst of the Mau Mau revolution in Kenya and the rising surge for independence throughout Africa. It was an exciting and dangerous time. In many ways prophetic. Both of them believed absolutely that it was God's will that they should go to Africa. They were guided by a blunt and uncomplicated code of service: Find a need and respond to it.

The impact they have had on literally hundreds of thousands of lives in Africa cannot be measured on any conventional scale of economic or social development. What they have done in their nearly fifty years of mission and care-giving was to take the parable of the Good Samaritan and invest it—each day of their lives—with energy and devotion that in ways large and small have changed the life of every African they served. In doing that, they also served us.

The monuments to that work fill the landscape of Tanzania: more than 2,500 one-room schools built primarily with money raised by Dave Simonson, his partners in Operation Bootstrap, and in hundreds of churches across America. Add to this the remarkable campus of the Maasai Girls' School at Monduli, built in cooperation with the Tanzanian government, the Lutheran Church, and the Maasai elders, on a coffee plantation that will someday provide most of the money to operate it; and the modern hospital at Selian, near Arusha, where Dave and Eunice once maintained a tiny commissary that gave free pills to the poor. That hospital at Selian has saved hundreds of lives and is a leader in the worldwide struggle to control AIDS.

Each morning for years, Eunice would get up to find fifteen to twenty African women sitting on benches outside their home. This was Eunice's Back Door Clinic, which became an institution in Tanzania. She gave what medicines she had. She gave water, advice, shelter when it was necessary, embraces, and friendship. Over the years, they came by the thousands. She was, simply, "Mama." No one was turned away. Later she flew with the Flying Doctors and learned to fly herself. She even became a passable anesthesiologist in that little hospital in Wasso. And you must remember, Eunice, the first patient you put under anesthetic—you, holding scissors for the doctor in one hand and, in the other hand, a manual on how to open those valves. And then you were somewhat astonished to see the operating doctor holding his own manual to learn what to do with an appendix. It was medicine in the bush.

And she also ministered to her husband who, over the years, was struck by anthrax twice, malaria numerous times, diabetes, cancer, a heart blockage, and a stroke last year. They almost died together in a light plane crash last year. David today shows the wear of that stroke. But this is an oak of man. I've never met one like him, in the power of his commitment, his utter belief that he is doing the work of God, and his undefeatable spirit. Dave's speech is impaired in the aftermath of the stroke, and he now needs a wheelchair, but next month they plan to return to their home in Tanzania to spend Christmas in Africa.

Mark Hanson mentioned Dave's struggle with bureaucracy. You should know that David Simonson, in his more intense moments, can be a load. He was a big guy, a football hero in college, a driven man in his mission. He has never considered himself qualified for sainthood. In her more candid moments, his wife may agree. If there were barriers, he knocked them down. If he couldn't knock them down, he found a way around them. In his first year as a missionary, the Maasai of a remote village asked if he could bring his LandRover and his shotgun to the edge of the village. A rogue lion was threatening to kill their cattle and menacing the children. David was a hunter in Minnesota, but he had never encountered a lion. He drove to the savanna in darkness. The lion appeared, roaring and advancing toward him. He trembled with the gun at his shoulder and fired. The lion fell dead. And the next day, there were a lot of villagers considering the virtues of becoming new Lutherans.

I remember walking 200 miles in the African Rift with Dave Simonson and other friends to raise money for those primary schools. We'd offer a small prayer at 5:30 in the morning and then start out. On this day we were walking through lion country, and we heard lions roaring nearby. David was not above dramatics now and then, a kind of white-collar Hemingway. He had two Ruger revolvers strapped to his hips. I fell in with him and talked tersely about prospects. "Reverend," I said, "do you think those revolvers can stop a lion?" He considered that for a moment. "Probably not," he said, "I've always felt that in tough spots the Lord will take care of me." I considered that for a moment. "Wonderful," I said, "But what about the rest of us?"

Somebody took care of us. Dave Simonson helped bring thousands of Africans to Christianity, yes. But that was not the central part of their mission. When we think of Africa today, we think in stereotypes—civil war, AIDS, corruption, genocide, poverty. There IS that, of course. But there is another Africa—the thousands of Africans who are living expanded lives of hope and self-respect today, knowing something about disease prevention, better-educated Africans, Africans who now feel they matter.

Many of them are Africans whose lives were and are part of the lives of David and Eunice Simonson. When you look at the mission of Dave and Eunice, you are moved to examine the grace of God. To look at their work and the beauty of their faith is to tell you: In the eyes of those they have served, their work flowed from the grace of God. And so it has. When they went to Africa, David and Eunice took with them an unbreakable faith, an unbreakable love for each other and for family, and a commitment to serve that never wavered. It is still there, glowing bright and strong, through illness, age, and the changing times, a faith that is a benediction for all of this. Because of this and so much more, they richly deserve the honor they receive tonight, deserve our admiration and our love.

We were privileged to meet Dr. Norman Borlaugh, American agronomist, Nobel Peace laureate, and father of the "green revolution". He was also being given the Wittenberg Award. What a wonderful, humble man.

Retirement

There comes a time in our "working" lives, when we are informed that "It's time." The many friends of our peer group write that they are more involved in life after retirement than ever before. A definition I once heard that fits this retirement— "re-tire—a new set of tires."

For us, this has been very true. Dave still had several big projects he wanted to complete, and the bishop was very happy

With Bishop Thomas Laiser and his wife, Maria

to have us continue. Our mission board informed us it was OK with them, and we would now live on pension, social security, love from friends, family, and God!

Dave felt many years before retirement that it might be wise to buy a house in America, should we be forced to leave Tanzania. We began sorting through the many "connections" and locations of where we should look. Dave's father, Rudolph Simonson, had come from an area near Fergus Falls. His mother, also a Simonson, had lived in Fergus Falls as a young child, where her father, Simon Christian Simonson (remember, the one who came to America from Gudbransdalen, Norway, around the same time my great grandfather, Christian Nordby came to America from the same town), was pastor at Bethlehem Lutheran Church. Dave's paternal aunt, Anna, had worked at the Fergus Falls City Hospital, and Dave was sent to her, at a time of difficulty in his family. He spent a year in Fergus Falls.

One more special "connection" was our dear friends' Richard and Chris (yes, my childhood "sister") Hefte were now living in Fergus Falls. Richard worked with a law firm and was very informed on many matters, including clients who intended to sell their homes.

Richard took Dave to meet Mr. Davenport, whose house he wished to sell, and they went to check it out. It was just perfect, and Dave knew I would love it. A small, wooden house, split level, on a high embankment overlooking the Red River Lake,

Our Fergus Falls house in the woods.

With friends Mary Johnson, Chris Hefte, Dorothy Skramstad, and Ruth Boe – on the deck of our Fergus Falls house.

part of Ottertail River. The land included two acres of woods, gardens, and even a vineyard. The house itself was designed by yet another "connection"—Charles Beck, one of Concordia's well-known artists, who also lives in Fergus Falls. There was no hesitation, and a contract of payment was signed. When I saw it the first time, I was also thrilled. Now we had two of the loveliest places in the world. My Norwegian guilt said, "You have too much."

While we only lived in this house on our trips to the States for speaking engagements and medical checks, it has been enjoyed and cared for by many. Our children enjoyed time there: Becky and Jim's wedding was held in Fergus Falls, and the family time after was at our River Heights home. Naomi has been living in it now, while she completes several higher degrees at Minnesota State University, Moorhead. It puts her close to her son, Seth, his wife, Amber, and her beautiful grandsons, Gavin and Grant, who live in Fergus Falls.

We became members of First Lutheran Church on one of our longer stays. Many lasting and precious friendships were formed. Dave was on speaking tours much of the time, and I enjoyed the Women's Bible Study group as well as speaking at local churches and schools. Pastor Saul Stensvaag has brought several groups of young people from First to Tanzania, which has

been life changing for many of these fine young people!

All these experiences restored us in many ways, yet we always were ready and eager to return to our hilltop home in Tanzania.

First Lutheran Church Fergus Falls youth group in Tanzania

The Rest of the Story

Most everyone of our age group will remember this line: "And now for the rest of the story." The newscaster, Paul Harvey, for many years ended each news broadcast with these words, then add some interesting background information. So, I use these words to end my story.

I have a prayer, written by a Mother Superior in the seventeenth century, hanging on the wall over my computer. As I read it often, I realize how quickly we aging women can be guilty of most of the "failings" she addresses. The years of 2000 seem filled with so many medical challenges; the temptation to "rehearse them" could fill yet another book.

Lord, you know better than I know myself that I am growing older and will someday be old. Keep me from getting talkative and particularly from the fatal habit of thinking that I must say something on every occasion.

Release me from craving to straighten out everybody's affairs. Keep my mind from the recital of endless details; give me wings to come to the point.

I ask for grace enough to listen to the tales of others' pains, but seal my lips on my own aches and pains—they are increasing, and my love of rehearsing them is becoming sweeter as the years go by. Help me to endure them with patience.

I dare not ask for improved memory, but for a growing humility and a lessening cocksureness when my memory seems to clash with the memories of others. Teach me the glorious lesson that occasionally it is possible that I may be mistaken.

Keep me reasonably sweet. I do not want to be a saint—some of them are so hard to live with—but a sour old woman is one of the crowning works of the devil.

Give me the ability to see good things in unexpected places, and talents in unexpected people. And give me, O Lord, the grace to tell them so.

Make me thoughtful, but not moody; helpful, but not bossy. With my vast store of wisdom it seems a pity not to use it all, but thou knowest, Lord, that I want a few friends at the end.

Amen.

I would rather share the amazing "God-incidents" that were given us as we moved from hospital to hospital.

The story of our plane crash in 2003 has been shared in an earlier chapter. Many God-incidents came with that experience. After coming to a full stop in a village cornfield, we were surrounded by villagers who recognized Dave as the one who had started their church and built their school. The loving care they gave us, with prayers and a strong support to me from a strong Maasai man, was truly given by God.

The medical team, Dr. Mark Jacobson and Dr. Paul Kisanga, when we reached Selian Hospital, gave us instant care—x-rays and pain medication given with deep love. Dr. Mark had called a thoracic surgeon at Nairobi Hospital to be on standby to care for me; my sternum was smashed and I was bleeding internally. A plane "just happened" to be available from Father Pat Patton and a nurse. I was well sedated, so the transport went well. The intended surgeon was not available when I arrived, so I asked for Dr. Gikonyo, the president's doctor, who had cared for Dave several times and was the only name I knew. The emergency room staff were amazed that I would ask for him, but they called him. He just happened to be in the hospital and came immediately. I felt this true God-incident again because of God's connection.

In July, when Dave and I were strong enough, we were advised to go to the States where further testing should be given Dave for his failing heart. Naomi was with us and provided much loving support. We were welcomed by our friend, Dr. Verce Fuglestad, who made all the arrangements for Dave to be admitted to Unity Hospital.

Dave's time at Unity was dramatic in many ways. There were several East African caregivers working on that floor, who came often to visit Dave and connect to their homeland; Swahili was the language of choice.

A Tanzania mission retreat was being held in St. Paul, so we were visited by dear friends. One day, as Dave was being discharged, Annette Stixrud (a close friend and former teacher of our children at Kiomboi) went with me to the cafeteria for a quick lunch. When we returned to the room, Dave was lying unconscious on the floor. Emergency action was taken, and he was rushed to ICU—a major stroke!

The weeks that followed were critical. The boys were called and came from Tanzania; Becky came from North Dakota. The prayers of the assembled missionaries, together with those of people around the world, were raised and answered. Dave lived, but was paralyzed on his right side and his speech was greatly affected. When he gained consciousness, he began speaking in Swahili, which the doctors didn't know; they thought he was just mumbling nonsense. We were there to help translate.

Much therapy was needed, so he was transferred to Sister Kenny Institute, where he was cared for by many fine people. Another connection here too—one of the therapists had been to Tanzania and enjoyed the time with Dave and me.

By September we were able to return to our Fergus Falls house on 24617 River Lake Heights Road. I always chuckle at this fancy address on a dead end, dirt road. How wonderful being home in this, our American home, reunited with our friends there. Actually, Dave was admitted to Lake Region Medical Center in Fergus Falls, where he received wonderful rehabilitation services in occupational therapy, physical therapy, and speech. I spent most nights with him; the kind staff let me stay in the empty bed in his room. Occasionally I would go home to Naomi and Seth, and have a shower and nap. Months later, Dave came home and the rehabilitation services were done on an outpatient basis.

Our doctor during this time in Fergus Falls was Dr. David Bjork, a missionary kid from Japan and a wonderful man! Dave continued to gain strength on his right side and was able to do some walking. We joined the YMCA and enjoyed the walks around their track. Naomi was our rock and Christ our Rock of Ages. We made friends with other regular walkers. In fact, a future "connection" was made, as one of the couples was the paternal grandparents of Amber, the girl that Seth would eventually marry.

We spent Christmas that year in the States, which enabled us to celebrate with Becky and family, who came to our house from western North Dakota. It was a rare treat to have so much time with our "American" grandchildren. I also was able to attend the Concordia College Christmas concert with Naomi, Seth, and Amber, his new fiancée—such an uplifting occasion.

The year 2004 was another medically challenging year for us. It was also a time of healing gifts. Dave was hospitalized several times with congestive heart failure. In addition to his medical needs, I collapsed and was brought into the emergency room in Fergus Falls. A series of procedures found that I had several consequences from our plane crash. My entire stomach had been forced into my thoracic cavity, through a hiatal hernia. This was the cause of my difficulty in breathing. Surgery followed, with the stomach being returned to its proper place; it was so good to be able to breathe again!

By April it was felt that Dave's heart condition needed the expert care of doctors at Mayo Clinic in Rochester, Minnesota. Referrals and appointments were made by Dr. Bjork and the next medical saga began. Dave's brother, Jim, was at Mayo, waiting for him to arrive. He escorted him to all his appointments. As a doctor, he was well acquainted with the procedures and the layout of Mayo.

Dave was sent to the cardiologist, Dr. Bruce, who received us warmly, especially when he learned we had an African "connection." He was from South Africa. After more tests, Dave was scheduled quickly for open heart surgery, to replace his aortic valve. The surgeon was Dr. Zehr, who was married to a missionary kid from Tanzania! He had done part of his residency at Shirati, a Mennonite mission hospital near Shinyanga. How is that for a "connection"! This is the same hospital at which Kris Hartwig worked.

The wonder of these "connections" continued when Dave had to have special x-ray and ultrasound procedures done; the woman doing these was a missionary kid from our missionary family in Tanzania! Charlotte Edstrom Siebenaler was also the sister of one of Naomi's high school roommates in Kenya.

One question was asked, "Do you want a pig's valve or a cow's valve?" The reply came without hesitation, "A cow's valve; I am a Maasai." When Naomi emailed this to some of the Tanzanian clergy, they all had a good laugh. Dave maybe even went up a notch in the estimation of these Maasai men by having a part of their sacred cows in him.

The surgeon told us that Dave's chances of surviving the surgery were not good. Dave's brothers and their wives—Luther and Audrey, Paul and Bonnie, James and Shirley—came, as did friends like Jim Klobuchar, Jim Nestingen, and the Heftes. The boys and Becky were not able to come, but Naomi and Seth were there. It was difficult, as we all said "Goodbye," and tears flowed as Dave was wheeled off to surgery. Naomi contacted a long list of friends and family and once again, there was a world-wide circle of prayer surrounding Dave and all of us who patiently waited for the outcome of the nine-hour surgery. How strengthened we all were, having family near, people praying, and a loving God!

This all went on during the week of Easter, and my favorite hymn, "Because he lives, I can face tomorrow," echoed in my heart as I celebrated this day of life, in the beautiful chapel of Mayo! Once again our lives were being restored. Dave, with God's powerful hand, beat the odds, and we met him up in the intensive care unit, where he stayed several days. During that time, they also put in a pacemaker to stabilize his heart.

Once out of intensive care, he was transferred next door to St. Mary's Hospital for rehabilitation. Another "connection"—the woman who came to do the physiotherapy had been on safari with Naomi!

I was able to find a nice room at an inexpensive hotel just across the street from St. Mary's, so was able to spend every day with Dave. Many visitors brought cheer and encouragement! The weeks passed quickly, and we were ready to return to Fergus Falls, where Dave was hospitalized once again in skilled nursing. By this time, we were well-known by the staff and

Some of the Maasai girls studying at Concordia College came to visit Babu (Maa meaning grandfather) while in the hospital.

welcomed back as family.

On April 24, Naomi and I went to Concordia to receive the Soli Deo Gloria Award, in recognition of the scholarship we set up for Maasai girls coming to Concordia each year. We heard a beautiful tribute by President Paul Dovre and Linda Brown, and received a large mosaic picture made with Venetian glass pieces saying "Soli Deo Gloria." I wished that Dave had been able to be there with me.

We were not finished with hospitals yet. Dave was admitted once again, this time as a result of hemorrhaging, needing transfusions. I had my days in hospital again too, when I was taken to the emergency room with a possible heart attack. After an ambulance ride to Fargo and multiple tests, I was able to return in a couple days with meds and instructions to rest—no heart attack.

This worked out well, as Dave was discharged and put on home care. The therapists, who had worked with him in rehab now came three days a week to the house. The links, friendships, and recovery were received with thankfulness.

The pattern of life throughout the summer was woven with visits from family and friends, medical checks, exercise at the YMCA, and times of anxiety and excitement. We found ourselves longing to return home to Tanzania, yet realizing this long period in our American home was truly a gift from God. Dave was somewhat stronger, so we began so make plans.

Naomi, who had been with us through all the challenges, was willing to go with us and did all the arrangements for travel. With Dave's fragile condition, extra requests needed to be made with airlines. When all seemed to be in place, we were ready to go.

On December 10, 2005, we bade farewell to all in Fergus Falls and went to Minneapolis for our KLM flight to Amsterdam. Jim and Shirley Simonson were at the airport, as were many friends, such as Herb Morgenthaler, John Pierce from Concordia, and Verce Fuglestad. They were given passes to sit with us until boarding—a nice bonus, considering all the restrictions post-9/11. We reached the halfway mark, just off the coast of Newfoundland before crossing the sea to Greenland, and the pilot informed us that they had lost a compass, so needed to return to Minneapolis. This was hard to hear, when we were holding our breath that Dave would survive the long flights to Tanzania.

Back at the Minneapolis airport, things were mayhem! Naomi took charge and went to work. At 2:30 a.m., we were given a hotel, and Naomi said she would deal with the airlines on the phone once she had put us to bed. We had to reclaim all our luggage, which as usual was the maximum allowed, and got a taxi. Good thing we raised a daughter with muscles! We arrived at the hotel and were told that they did not have any wheelchairs, something we were told there would be. Naomi quickly grabbed a big luggage trolley, piled all our luggage onto it, perched Dave on top of the luggage, set his black hat on his head, told him to hold on, and off we went. We looked a sight! Naomi took the corner to the elevator at a squeal, and we were all giggling like little kids. Even Dave was having a good time! We were tucked in bed and asleep in no time. Naomi went to her room and spent the rest of the early morning on the phone with the airline, making alternative plans for the coming day.

We made the trip without any further delays or problems. Thank God!

People in My Life

Our Kids, Grandkids, and Great-grandkids

STEPHEN DANIEL, born August 1, 1953, in Fairview Hospital, Minneapolis, Minnesota, while Dave was still at Luther Seminary and I (until two weeks before his birth) was working in Miller Hospital in St. Paul, as surgical nurse. Steve gave us such excitement, as a child of curiosity and adventure.

After graduating from Concordia College in Moorhead, Minnesota, he returned to Tanzania, married Marilyn Shaffer, and moved to the Hurri Hills of northern Kenya, where he worked for Lutheran World Relief as a conservationist. They were the only permanent people there, as the Gabra were nomadic and would come through from time to time on their

Steve's family – front: Serena, Marilyn, Arlene; back: Lane, Steve, Caleb

camels. Their first three children—Serena, Arlene, and Caleb—were born during this time. These were very happy times for them.

They then moved down to live in Nairobi, Kenya, for two years, while Steve attended the university and received his masters in business administration. The girls began horseriding lessons while still in the Hurri Hills, and when they moved to Nairobi were soon taking many ribbons at the horse shows. Marilyn has been a strong support all these years—living in desert areas (for a time just in tents), teaching, and adjusting to many moves and lifestyles. Her Shaffer genes made themselves known; her love of Africa, Steve, family, and God continue to sustain and bless her (and us). Lane was born at the time they were moving to Tanzania.

When Steve and brothers, Nate and Jon, decided to put down roots in Tanzania, they started a safari company—Serengeti Select Safaris Ltd., and a lodge, Tarangire Safari Lodge, in Tarangire National Park. At present Steve and Nate are operating the safari business, and Jon and Annette are operating the lodge business.

Steve and Marilyn's children were all born, raised, and educated through high school in Africa.

Serena Marie, born February 24, 1981, is a graduate of Wellesley in Boston, received a Fulbright scholarship to Morocco, a masters degree in international relations from the University of Sussex, England. She was employed by Tanganyika Christian Refugee Services, working with Rwandan refugees. She has just been offered a position with Lutheran World Federation, Geneva, to work for them in a northern Kenyan refugee camp.

Arlene Elizabeth, born June 30, 1983, is a graduate of Rocky Mountain College in Billings, Montana. Her great love of horses determined her choice of equine studies. After three years of working in the U.S., she is now using her knowledge and love of horses in Tanzania, running her own stable of eighteen horses, teaching riding to over fifty children.

Caleb Daniel, born December 3, 1985, had attended California Lutheran University for two years and is now graduating from University of New Mexico, Albuquerque, New Mexico, with a biology major. An excellent actor and funny guy, he is also a superb rugby player. He has raced motocross since the age of five. He is married to his Dutch high school sweetheart, Heleen Van de Vijver.

Lane David, born June 13, 1990, joined his brother in Albuquerque and is enjoying studies in diesel mechanics. He was the toddler always using pulleys and other contraptions to make things work better. Also, like his brother, he is very competitive in rugby and motocross.

NAOMI RUTH, born November 23, 1954, (named after the sister of Dave who died shortly after birth) an adorable little red-head, who showed us very early in her life that she had a mind of her own. This strong characteristic has served her very well, but at times put her in trouble. She defines herself, as the "black sheep" of the family and on occasion tried to prove that, but her "other side" of loving concern always won out. She did get herself suspended from Rift Valley Academy when she sneaked out of the dorm one night to visit some boys in their dorm, for chai. A jealous girlfriend of one of the guys found out and squealed. She says that the administration called her in and had her off campus fast, before she could see any of her peers. She thinks it was so that she couldn't incite a riot; her nickname was "Napoleon" after all.

Naomi's family – Amber, Gavin, Seth, Naomi, and
Grant August (Inset)

She has a good mind and many gifts—a fine voice, a great
actress who starred in many theater productions, and has a
strong spirit of justice. Art and music are also her talents, although she has not had much time to use them. Many stories can
be told about these gifts used in creative ways! Her passion now
is photography.

She has had the opportunity to do many different types of
work over the years. After graduating from Concordia College in
1978 with a degree in psychology, she had her first position as a
counselor for emotionally and mentally challenged children at
Lake Park Wild Rice Children's Home, a Lutheran Social Service
program, in Fergus Falls, Minnesota. She enjoyed this, but after
three years was feeling burnt out. She applied for graduate
school and went back to Tanzania to wait for acceptance. During
this time, she became involved briefly with a missionary kid.
When she headed back to start graduate school in Idaho, she
stopped in India, where she had been invited to observe and
partake in a program for schizophrenics. After one month, she
discovered she was pregnant; the second month was spent in
hospital and bed after she almost lost the baby. When she was
given the OK by the doctor to travel, she flew back to the States.

The stories of living with schizophrenics, especially during her bedridden state, are enough to give you the heebie jeebies.

She stayed with the Bertelsens, friends of the family, who opened their hearts and home to Naomi while she was waiting to deliver. I went to the States for the birth, the hardest delivery I have ever witnessed, but the end results were wonderful—such a precious baby! I stayed with her at another home, where she would take care of two other little ones as payment for room. After a month and Seth's baptism, I returned to Tanzania. When Seth was eight months old, they moved back to Tanzania where she taught first grade teacher for two years at St. Constantine's School in Arusha.

From there she went on to be the manager of Gibb's Farm near Karatu, Tanzania, a quaint, beautiful tourist lodge amidst a coffee plantation near Ngorongoro Crater. She later served as manager of Serengeti Select Safaris for her brothers and as ground staff at Kilimanjaro International Airlines for KLM Royal Dutch Airlines. In 1989 she went back to the U.S. to be Africa travel specialist for a series of three different travel agencies that needed their Africa department either developed or improved. A year after sending Seth back to his father, Erik Rowberg, in Arusha (because as a soon to be teenager, he was open to some of the negative influences in the States), she moved back to Tanzania to work on-site for one of the travel agencies and also to help Serengeti Select Safaris. Later, while still helping them, she managed the Arusha offices for Gibb's Farm and Ndutu Safari Lodge, all tourism based.

In 2002, when Seth graduated from International School Moshi, in their international baccalaureate program, she decided to head back to school, as he started college. He started Concordia College, and Naomi began graduate studies in school psychology next door at Minnesota State University, Moorhead. The next year, after our plane crash and beginning of convalescence in the States, they both moved to Fergus Falls to live with us and help us. Naomi continued to take care of us while continuing a scaled down, prolonged version of her studies in Moorhead. She still remains in our house in Fergus Falls and is hopefully finishing her third degree this coming year—a masters degree in school psychology, a masters degree in special education almost complete, and a specialist degree in school psychology done after an internship. It has taken a long time to complete all these with the interruptions of flying back and forth, taking care of us.

Her ever-present presence in our times of need is immeasurable; our dear Naomi has been with us on every occasion of need (and these have been many). This "black sheep" wears the garments of white wool! With all the flights back and forth between the U.S. and Tanzania, she calls herself a jet-setter.

Seth Erik, born January 6, 1983, has given us such joy and thanksgiving. One of his great joys in life has been racing motocross. After the one year at Concordia, he moved to Fergus Falls with Naomi, to help us. Seth did a year at the Community College in Fergus Falls. The beautiful "connection" there was meeting and marrying Amber Peasley. I attended their wedding. Another "connection"—the officiating pastors at First Lutheran Church were Matt and Amy Larson, who had served in Tanzania at the girls' school and became like family to us. Seth and Amber continued studies at Minnesota State University, Moorhead, while living in Fargo, North Dakota, then moved back to Fergus Falls to live. Seth started his own company for parts and accessories for motorsports, B SS Powersports, and works with his father-in-law, Larry Peasley, at his car dealership. Amber is a speech pathologist, a dedicated Christian who has blessed Seth in many ways. The birth of their first child, **Gavin David**, on September 26, 2007, is the joy of all—our first great-grandchild. Seth is now studying again, to become a civil engineer-surveyor, at North Dakota School of Science in Wahpeton.

Grant August, born November 1, 2010. What a sweetie he is!

NATHAN DAVID, born January 26, 1956, in Market Harborough, England during our six-month stay in England while Dave was studying at the University of London. The biggest of our children (ten pounds at birth and 6"4" now), Nathan is blessed with quiet dignity and strength. At three weeks of age, he survived the move to Africa.

Like his brother and sister, he went to Concordia College for two years, then transferred to North Dakota State University, Fargo, North Dakota, to graduate in civil engineering. Both Steve and Nate were given a "home away from home" during

Nathan's family – Luke, Bethany, Susan, Nathan, Daniel

these years at the home of their Uncle Paul (Dave's brother) and Aunt Bonnie Simonson. They were given much love and good jobs at Uncle Paul's automated maintenance business.

When Nate returned to Tanzania, he found work with Tanganyika Christian Refugee Services in Singida, central Tanzania, with a water development project. He was then sent to Mishamo, in western Tanzania, to work with Rwandan refugees. There he met Susan Down, who was with the medical unit of the program. A great match for Nate, Susan is Canadian but with a truly international background. Born in Namibia, with a childhood in Ireland, nurses training in Canada, Susan received a masters degree in public health in Hawaii, worked among the natives of northern Canada, and then came to Tanzania. Nate and Susan were married in Tarangire, beside a Baobab tree. As the children came, they were each baptized by this same tree. Nate was hired by Lutheran World Federation in Geneva, and their first posting was in Lindi, Tanzania. We laughed at this, because it seems that all misbehaving government officials get sent to Lindi. Daniel was born there. Their next posting was Mozambique, where both Luke and Bethany were born. We were blessed to have been able to visit them in Mozambique and in South Africa where they were later stationed.

At this time in Nathan's career, Dave's health began to fail. The building of the Maasai Girls School (MGLSS) was nearing completion, but Dave was finding the work too difficult. Nate recognized this and offered to come back to Tanzania to complete the project. Such an amazing gift! We will never forget this. He has been there for us in so many ways. Susan has been there to support and raise the three children. They lived with us for four years, so our life was enriched in many ways. They now live on the top of the hill above us.

Daniel Richard, born November 29, 1991, has had the opportunity of living in three African countries. A brilliant student and athlete, he attends Queens university in Canada

Luke David, born November 8, 1993, is a young man of charm and many gifts—athlete, actor, and a willing helper to all of us.

Bethany Euella (combination of the two grandmothers— Eunice and Donella), born September 5, 1995, is my "Sweet Pea." An adorable teenager now, Bethany's love of children will definitely be a determining passion in her future. As our youngest granddaughter, she has received extra love and attention, and she thrives on it.

REBECCA MARIE was born February 7, 1958. I have written the "miracle" story of our Becky and wish to add an update on the five grandchildren that she and Jim have given us. We do not have the opportunity to see them often, but visits either for me to the States or Becky returning with parts of her family here to Tanzania, we have seen them.

David Lloyd, born May 16, 1985, has joined Jim and his six brothers in their large ranching/farming enterprise. He is a big, strong young man, capable of all tasks this lifestyle requires. He has a beautiful singing voice that he shares with the church, often singing at family weddings. His quiet gentle demeanor can hide the strength he has been given.

Stephanie Marie was born November 4, 1986. A lovely young lady, Stephanie graduated from Concordia College and from the college in Williston, North Dakota. She is a physical therapist assistant in Dickenson, North Dakota. As an eight year old, she assumed an adult role in caring for Becky after brain

Rebecca's family — front: Rebecca and Jim; back: Anthony, David, Kristina, Lloyd, Stephanie

surgery, taking the responsibility of helping raise her younger siblings. She is a woman of strength and compassion, a singer and a self-taught guitarist as well. She did extremely well in athletics throughout high school but chose to concentrate on academics when she went to college.

Kristina Violet, born February 21, 1991, could easily be a model with striking beauty. Being very little at the time of Becky's recovery was very hard on her, and she remains a quiet, shy young lady. She is also athletic and smart, like her sister. She was at North Dakota State University in Fargo, North Dakota. She has applied to the dental assistant program in Whapeton.

Lloyd James, born January 21, 1994, is a quiet young man. A good student who has gone to state competitions several times, he has grown tall and has a good record in all sports. He is the redhead in their family.

Anthony Simon, born September 13, 1995, is the miracle child whose life could have been taken when, at three months inter-uteral, Becky was warned that all the medicines, anesthesias, and traumas could harm or kill this fetus. How gracious was God in saving this perfect baby! He is outstanding in every way—intelligent and another great athlete.

JONATHAN PAUL, was born June 12, 1961. Our fifth child from God deserves a chapter—an adventurous child, mechanical genius, a *rafiki* (friend) of all his African buddies.

He loved riding his motorcycle that he had rebuilt. He was a careful driver, obeying all the traffic rules. However, a transforming and tragic event when he was sixteen caused this carefree teenager to change to a serious, industrious adult.

Jon spent his junior and senior high school years in the mission school of Ft. Dauphin in Madagascar. There he met and fell in love with Annette Lellelid. She was thirteen years old when he told her that one day he would marry her, and he did. Another God "connection": Annette's parents, Leo and Renie Lellelid, had gone to Madagascar from Luther Seminary before we left for Africa.

Jon and Annette married July 19, 1986, at the mission apartments in St. Paul, with mission friends from both Madagascar and Tanzania joining with our families. A very happy reunion and union! Together they returned to Tanzania and have been transforming the Tarangire tented camp and lodge into one of the favorite places for countless visitors. Together with Steve and Nate, they have formed a great travel team. They then went on to purchase a beautiful piece of Indian Ocean front land, where they have built a lodge (Emayani Beach Lodge) and later added the property next door that already had *bandas* for guests (Tulia Beach Lodge). Jon and Annette are a great team. Their two

Jonathan's family – Annette, Sophie, Brenden, Jon

children have had the joy of living among the animals of Tarangire and the seascape of Emayani.

Sophia Arlene, born March 13, 1990, is now studying hotel management in New Zealand. She will do well with her winsome personality and conscientious attitude. These qualities are attributed to her mom's gifts.

Brenden Jon, born October 27, 1992, has inherited his dad's mechanical skills and charm. He is also an avid bird watcher like his dad. (So is Sophie.)

Missionaries and Missionary Kids

One of the most special parts of being on the mission field, is the unique and wonderful experience of being part of the mission family. This is a "family" that grows together through good times and bad, and sustains us even when we are physically distant from one another. We are a family in Christ. Our mission "family" was a closely-knit group of people here with a same purpose—to proclaim the Good News. When we came to Tanganjika under the American Lutheran Church (Norwegian in background), we found most of our collegues were from the Swedish Lutheran background, most of them working in central Tanzania. The connecting link was often through our children who attended the same mission schools. These bonds were strongly knit at Kiomboi, where they were lovingly cared for at the mission school, by 'parents' like Fred and Martha Malloy and later Roy and Inez Philpot. Many went on together to Rift Valley Academy in Kenya for high school.

In the hierarchy of the "family," some of the older missionaries became mentors, "moms" and "dads" to the more newly arrived missionaries. Those in our own age range were not only friends, but some also became like "brothers" and "sisters." Our children grew up referring to the parents of their friends as "uncle" and "aunt." The children bonded with a feeling of "brothers" and "sisters." By spending years away at boarding schools together, these bonds have lasted forever. For some of those missionary kids who have stayed on in Tanzania and are raising their families here, our grandchildren have experienced the same extension of mission "family" and the feeling of being "siblings."

The loving support of fellow missionaries has meant so much to us throughout these years. The first mission news we received from Stan on arrival in Nairobi was that Elder and Renee Jackson had twin girls, Martha and Deborah, just days before in Karatu, near Ngorongoro Crater. They were so little that they kept them in the oven. I was so amazed and wondered if that was a common practice. Dean, Joel, and Kim were "brothers" to our boys, and Beth, Martha, Deborah, and Jill were "sisters" to our girls. We had many great times with the Jacksons over the years.

The Palms (Harold and Evelyn) were some of the first missionaries we met when we arrived at Marangu, and their son, Eugene (Ugi), was one of Steve's buddies through Kiomboi, Rift Valley Academy, and after. Beatrice and Duane were slightly older, but they were still a part in our children' lives.

Dean and Elaine Peterson's boys, Dave, Thad, and Mike, are all living in Arusha, working in tourism, and they remain very close to our three boys, Steve, Nate, and Jon, who also work in tourism. These families have extended the missionary "family," with all of their children being best friends and "siblings" from the time they were born. The six boys do an annual "Old Boy" safari together, where they invite a few other guys to join them for several days out in the bush. There is a feeling of being privileged to be invited into this bastion of brotherhood.

Les and Ruth Peterson (brother of Dean) were in central Tanzania, so our contact was mainly through our kids. Luella and Rachel were older than our children, so Marilyn (who later married fellow missionary kid, Pete Friberg), Bobbie Lu, and Paul were the ones more closely related to our kids.

Dan and Ruth Friberg were the most beautiful examples of Christian committed people I had ever met. "Auntie Ruth" was like a big sister to me and, even though we did not have much time together, I hoped to be like her. Their eldest daughter, Margaret (Mugsie), spent time with us in Loliondo and gave us such joy. Their boys, David (Pete), Steve, and John, were close friends with our boys. Their Steve became a pediatrician and now works out among the Maasai, so we get to see him and his family occasionally. The older children, Joe, Margaret and Mary, seemed to become closer to us as they became adults. When Naomi and Seth lived in Minneapolis, they became a close part of the Friberg family who now live in Minneapolis after their time in Tanzania. They spent much time, including holidays like Thanksgiving and Christmas, with the Fribergs. Today Naomi stays with "Auntie Ruth" (her second mother) when she visits Minneapolis. "Brother Joe" has come to her aid many times. The feeling of "family" continues.

Ray and Nellie Faye Hagberg lived in the mission house next to ours in Ilboru. There was lots of sharing between Nellie Fay and me as we were both expecting babies (Rochelle and Jon). Ray was working most of the time. They had three children— Lynnae, Rochelle, and Vaughn.

Ray and Gloria Cunningham lived in a remote area, but we got to know them through the children and missionary get-togethers. Diane, Patty, and Steve were part of our children's lives at school. Their Steve is now a pilot living in Arusha with his family, so he continues to be a part of our family. Dave was honored to perform his marriage.

Hal and Louise Faust worked in the same general area as the Cunninghams. We would sometimes take part of our vaca-tions and visit both families. Mark, Ann, and Linda were slightly older than our kids, but their Steve was in Naomi's class and David was in Beckys. They always enjoyed their times together.

Stan and Marie Benson have always been a close part of our family, as they are blood family as well as mission "family." John, Todd, and Jeff still are closely entwined with our kids. Naomi has been doing graduate studies at Minnesota State University, Moorhead, where John is a professor; he was part of her thesis committee. Todd is married to Betsy, our daughter-in-law Marilyn's sister, and connected with the Shaffer family.

Paul Bolstad was a missionary kid who grew up in the Usambara Mountains and returned to Arusha as a teacher in the 1970s. We became close with his wife, Shirley, and their children Sarah (our godchild) and Christopher, and, when they returned to the States, Laura. Paul went into real estate and helped Naomi find a house in Minneapolis.

Also in the 1970's, Poul and Susanna Bertelsen came to Arusha. Dave started an organization called MSAADA (Multi-sector Architectural Assistance for Developing Africa) and Poul, as an architect, stepped in to run it and still operates it today in Wayzata, Minnesota. Their children came along at the same time as the Bolstad children: Kennet, Marian (our godchild), and Nathan (Naomi's godchild).

Missionary kids are known to be unique in many ways. Prof. John Benson (son of Marie and Stan) has written a thesis on these "third culture" kids. The "third culture" label is given because our kids come from the culture of their parents (U.S.A.), live in another culture (Tanzania); from those two cultures they blend their own culture, the third culture. It is a term not only for missionary children, but for any child of one culture living in another culture ie, military children, immigrants. This whole field is very interesting, and the children very unique. Naomi says "the whole world is our playground." These kids who grew up in a new culture became international through their many school-mates and had the joy of belonging to a greater "family" than most. Those who grew up here in Tanzania lived in an Eden paradise and moved freely with the wonderful African people.

We became each others family and these dear ones still call us "Auntie Euni" and "Uncle Dave." We always were pleased when these kids would come home with ours— on safari trips, choir tours, rugby tournaments, and just for a change in scene. At Loliondo, we had visits from most of the mission family; we were in such a good place.

We also encountered some of these kids when going through the medical events in America. Mim Monson was surgical nurse who assisted at Becky's surgery; Char Edstrom did the ultrasounds on Dave at Mayo.

There are many other mission families that I may have neglected to mention, but this doesn't lessen their importance in our 'family'. I wrote this chapter mainly remembering things through my children's experiences and their "siblings." I am getting old and do not always remember everything. For this I apologize if I hurt anyone's feelings.

Fruits of the Writing Academy

Twenty-third Psalm

This wonderful Psalm has brought solace and strength to so many people. Today, as I reflect on these precious words, with my newly-broken leg elevated on a pillow and supported by a cast, they cause me to recall vividly another time.

Some twelve years ago, Dave and I were on furlough in America. Dave had been on a very intense speaking tour, with little rest. We were on our way to yet another engagement when Dave was forced to stop the car and pull over into a side road. As I watched him, breathless and struggling for air, I realized he was having a heart attack. I managed to get him to the nearest emergency room, where he was seen and cared for by a cardiologist.

Tests showed that Dave had complete blockages in five vessels that would require immediate surgery. With surgery scheduled, I contacted the family. Together we placed him in God's hands. With the combination of God's blessings and skillful surgeons, the crisis passed.

As he recovered, a Pastor Donaldson came often to pray and share God's word with Dave. This was of great comfort to both Dave and me. On one occasion, he shared thoughts on the Twenty-third Psalm. When reading the phrase, "He maketh me to lie down in green pastures," I had always envisioned the Shepherd bringing his flock into a lovely green meadow, for comfort and enjoyment. Pastor Donaldson shared a new and very interesting interpretation. In the days of David, a shepherd sometimes needed to deal harshly with the lead sheep or goat, so that it would not lead the flock into danger, but rather lead them where they could lie down and rest in green pastures—even if that meant breaking the leg of the lead animal.

God, at times, allows his children to be restricted for a while, so that their souls may be *restored*. How often in our serving or leading, we fail to allow ourselves to rest *in God's green pastures* and neglect to take time to follow and be led *in the path of righteousness.*

The doctors tell me I must not put weight on this broken leg. I must rest completely. Like the busy sheep or goat, I have been made to lie down. Now the restoration of my soul and body can proceed *in the path of righteousness.*

My cup runneth over. When word of my fall and broken leg went out, the love and prayers came in. Within a few minutes, after I was able to call our son, Nathan, he and his wife Susan were at our house. They, in turn, called the three beloved doctors (Mark Jacobson, Kris Hartwig, and Ron Eggert) who came quickly. Three doctors making house calls! Wow, such service! Each checked and agreed, there was a broken bone, and Nathan carefully drove me to our Selian Hospital where Dr. Mark had called in orders for x-rays and care by the orthopedic doctor, Dr. Kibera. Because I had been an integral part of this hospital's inception, I was welcomed and cared for by many dear co-workers, with prayers offered by several. The wonderful staff made me comfortable for my return home. Many others came into my room to offer *"pole sanas"* and prayers for my healing. Several laid hands of healing prayers on my leg. I was showered with love from friends and family who came all day to express their love and concern. Truly, my cup overflowed!

Yea though I walk through the valley of the shadow of death, I will fear no evil. Having started on this great Psalm, my thoughts and remembrances find each verse so applicable to me. Perhaps having been given a long life, so rich in accumulated experiences, allows me to fully appreciate how the words can be understood in so many ways. Death is not to be feared, when we are in God's grace and love. The shadow, that covers us at those times of losing loved ones, are often (for me) times of greater need for God's "rod and staff" than at other times. I have been near death on several occasions: a car accident when I was a teenager, severe hepatitis, an emergency hysterectomy, and an airplane crash. God's care through these medical emergencies and his will have brought me through these valleys. Facing the possible death of Dave has been hard, even though he is also in

God's care. Life is a precious gift and made even greater when in the shadow of his love. He is with me. His rod and staff they comfort me.

Thy rod and thy staff they comfort me. As I reflect on the Psalm, my thoughts have not always seen the rod as a comfort, but rather a sign of discipline. Perhaps through a theologian, all the significance of this could be explained. The proverb, "Spare the rod and spoil the child" is what some may feel as physical punishment. But I see it as the loving care in obedience to authority. A sheep would see it as protection against an attack of wild animals. We, too, are protected by God's power and made strong to withstand an attack from Satan.

In paintings of the Good Shepherd, he is always carrying the staff, with a lamb in the crook of his right arm or a sheep on his shoulder. In one painting of the Good Shepherd, he is rescuing a lamb that has fallen into a ravine, He is using the staff to reach the lamb. As Christ leads, he also has a hand and staff out-stretched to all of us, to offer comfort.

Savior, like a shepherd, lead us,
Much we need Thy tender care.
In thy pleasant pastures feed us,
For Your use our souls prepare.

As David and I planned our wedding, I requested this precious hymn for our processional, rather than the traditional wedding march. Now, fifty-seven years later, I have been made to lie down; the Shepherd Psalm and our wedding processional have come to take on a renewed meaning.

Truly, from the time I was a newborn lamb until this day as an aging ewe, my Shepherd has led me and provided many and varied pastures for me. Granted, I have wandered and placed myself in rocky places, but with the Shepherd's rod and staff, I have been returned, nourished and restored.

They Come to Our door

They come to our door
Weak, hungry and poor.
Too often their tears
Fall on cold hardened ears.
Some have nowhere to go,
No one willing to show
That the Lord has a place
To find love and God's grace.
We are told every day
As we read and we pray,
That the reason we're here
Is to bring love and cheer,
To care for our neighbors
And thank God for the favors
He so lovingly supplies,
To dry tears from their eyes.
God help me!

Three-legged Stool

The Maasai people of East Africa are noted for their ability to survive—spiritually, physically, and socially. All gain their strength from relationships.

A Maasai elder had agreed to share his wisdom of tribal traditions and knowledge with some university students. He welcomed them into his *boma* (village), where he seated them outside his hut. Each student was given a stool to sit upon, similar but smaller than that of the elder. The students asked many questions, and they were solemnly answered by the elder. When one young man asked, "How do the Maasai feel about relationships?" the old man's eyes shone, as he stood and lifted his three-legged stool, above his head. Pausing, to collect his thoughts, he resembled a prophet seeking wisdom from beyond.

"Look at this stool," he said, "It is carved out of a single piece of wood. Now, consider, it has three legs." The students wondered where all this would lead, but they realized they were about to learn something of great importance. The old man went on to explain, "The stool, because it is of one piece (of wood), represents wholeness. The three legs are vital because with fewer, the stool would not stand." Using the stool as an object lesson, he went on to explain the Maasai understanding of a relationship. "To achieve wholeness," he said, "three relationships must be intact."

The first and foremost leg represents the relationship to God. The Maasai believe in one creator God, who must be appeased and honored. The first milking of the day must be thrown heavenward. Prayers are offered for rain, fertility, and healing, as well as other needs. The Maasai traditionally believe that the cattle of the earth were given to them by God. Prayers of thanksgiving and praise are offered for this and for all good things.

Relationships with their fellow man are represented by the second leg. A close kinship exists between the several clans of the Maasai. Strict rules regarding marriage between clans maintain a pure tribe. Courtesy is given to strangers. Broken relationships need to be mended. The medicine man, before inquiring about a patient's ailments, will often ask, "With whom have you quarreled?"

The third leg represents the relationship to the environment. The Maasai are often considered the environmental caretakers in East Africa. These nomadic people will not allow their herds to overgraze an area when they are free to move about. They co-exist with the wild game, thus preserving large tracts of land. The government has set aside much of this land for national parks and game reserves. Because Maasai eat only the meat of their cattle, goats, and sheep, they will not be poachers. A reverence for God's creation defines this relationship.

The students left with a realization that they had learned more than Maasai traditions. They had received a lesson on life.

Christmas

"Only five more days 'til Christmas, Nana!" Bethany, the youngest of our granddaughters, exclaimed. We were doing our traditional decorating, and the grandkids were busy cutting snowflakes out of paper, to put on our windows. They would add a hint of a northern Christmas, in our tropical African setting. It was a bright and cheerful time, marred only by the failing health of Papa/Baba/Dave. His strength was failing, and blood loss was the cause. We brought this to the attention of our dear doctor friend, Mark Jacobson, who felt that testing and hospitalization was necessary.

On the day before Christmas Eve, Dave's blood pressure began to drop significantly, and he grew very weak. His hemoglobin dropped, and he was passing blood. Dr. Mark started him on IVs, but he felt that blood transfusions would be required soon, so he asked that our son, Steve, bring in donors. Steve came with his wife, Marilyn, son, Caleb, and friends, Trude and Ginny. After testing and cross-matching, the three women were compatible, and a reserve of blood was ready for transfusion. Most hospitals in Tanzania do not have blood available, so this was a substantial gift.

Unbeknownst to us, a Maasai mother was brought to Selian Hospital that night. She had miscarried and was near death from bleeding. Her hemoglobin was 1.0. Dr Jacobson had never seen anyone live with that reading. The miracle began when the blood available for Dave was compatable for her. She was given the blood and lived. Dave began to recover, without the given blood. The gift was placed in God's hand, and he chose to restore life to both the Maasai woman and to Dave—a Christmas gift we will long remember.

Beautiful Feet

"Do you have beautiful feet?" asked the pastor, as he began his sermon for the Sunday. One man replied, "Not bad, except for the fungus." A woman looked at her elegant feet, which had been carefully treated and the nails had been brightly polished, "Nice!" Some of us thought of our corned and bunioned feet, "Ugly!"

But, of course, the intention of the question was directed to how we use our feet. Do we use them to bring the Good News of salvation to others? Do we help those in need?

My thought went to my African mama, Mama Mesiaki. She had become our spiritual mama when we, as a young family, came as missionaries to Tanzania some fifty years ago. As she prayed each morning, she asked God, "Who needs our help this day?" As she listened, she responded by packing her basket with a thermos of *chai* (tea with milk and sugar), her Bible, and her hymnbook. She sometimes walked miles to minister to those needing help and guidance. On many occasions, I received her love and care. She continued this life of service until those blessed feet no longer could take her. But her prayers continued and gave blessing.

"Do you have beautiful feet?"

"How beautiful are the feet of those who bring Good News" (Isaiah 52:7).

"How beautiful are the feet of those who preach the Good News, proclaim peace, bring glad tidings of good things!" (Romans 10:15b).

Count Your Many Blessings

As I regained consciousness, in the intensive care unit of the Nairobi Hospital in Kenya, the soft, gentle voice of the nurses aide reached me. She was singing, "Count Your Many Blessings." There could not have been a more fitting reminder.

I was alive! A few days previously, this gift of life was in crisis, following an airplane crash in neighboring Tanzania. My husband, the pilot, and three others had survived as well, but I was considered critical and flown to Nairobi.

Reflecting on all of this and the countless blessings of our forty-eight years as missionaries to Tanzania kept my memory spinning. With each remembrance came the overwhelming feeling of thankfulness. It shouldn't take a dramatic experience to bring all these things to mind. Each day is a gift, a blessing— the embrace of a loved one, a kind word from a friend, the smile of a child, an assurance of care when needed, the beauty of God's creation—the list is endless.

Count your many blessings,
Name them one by one.
And it will surprise you,
What the Lord has done.

"O give thanks unto the Lord for he is good and his mercy endureth forever" (Psalm 107:1).

My Backdoor Bench

The mother and child sit quietly on the bench outside my back door. Their clothes are worn; the child's one piece of cloth barely covers his emaciated body. He reaches through the torn neckline of his mother's dress to pull on the empty breast, in hopes of nourishment as well as security. His eyes are large, his tummy distended, and he looks from me to his mother, as if trying to make some connection between us.

After the customary greetings, the mother says, "We have great hunger." There is no explanation, and I don't need one. She and her child are in great need.

An old woman with a wizened and wrinkled face, sits on my bench several days a week. She, too, is hungry. I know her story, of being abandoned by the death of her entire family. She sits patiently, with a forlorn attitude, waiting to be fed.

A man, who once worked with us and became like a brother, has had his life destroyed by the demon drink.

A child with an older brother waits for some medical attention. He was climbing a tree to collect honey and fell. His arm is carefully wrapped in a torn cloth, but the pain he feels from his broken wrist is intense, and he can barely keep the tears from falling.

My backdoor bench is seldom empty; as I meet each one my heart hurts. A prayer soars heavenward, seeking guidance. Food, clothing, medicines are always needed, but these must come with the assurance that God loves them. I love them, because Christ first loved me.

A Maasai neighbor brings her baby to my backdoor 'clinic'

Sunrise Symphony

Before the African equatorial sun has begun to paint the rift horizon with crimson and gold, the stage is being set. Even before nocturnal animals have sought out their dens, birds and creatures of the day are waking and assembling for their orchestral opening. The first chair oboe, the white-browed coucal, rings out repeatedly its single note. Mourning and ring-necked doves pick up the note and begin their hauntingly beautiful flute cadence. A discordant sound of the go-away birds creates tension, as the strings tune up. Piping piccolo trills of warblers, together with the percussion beats of quail and sand grouse, add volume and variety. Elephant's trumpet blast announces the brass, while the staccato beat of wildebeests' hooves, as they race to the river, set the tempo. A zebra barks— the director has given the word. The orchestra is ready as the curtains of night are drawn back. The Sunrise Symphony begins.

Purple Prelude

The African sun continues to parch the dry earth. Fissures and dust take over once-green landscape. Termites burrow out of the deep, creating passages of mud-lined walls which quickly dry in the relentless heat. Lethargy creeps into the lives of man and beast. Months of drought, have caused rivers to dwindle and streams to dry up completely. Hunger and despair consume many. Remembering the cycle of life creates hope for others, "For every season, turn, turn, turn . . ." The rains will come, in due season.

God has given wondrous signs that add strength to that hope. The heralding of life-restoring rain comes with the Purple Prelude. Each bush or plant with purple blooms responds to the preamble. Magnificent jacaranda trees that had looked lifeless, suddenly burst into lavender loveliness. Petrea bushes thrust out purple wands of flowers. Amid the dry grass, tiny purple aster-like flowers appear. Why purple, the color we associate with Lent? The season of suffering and the death of our Lord is the season of hope. It restores us through the outpouring of Christ's love to life.

McAllister Wedding

Dr. John "Jack" McAllister, a neurosurgeon, came to Tanzania with a group of doctors who were invited to become a part of the development of Selian Hospital. We were very involved, as Dave had instigated this project, and we became friends with Jack and others.

This friendship has brought Jack back to Tanzania many times, some of them with his lovely wife, Jane. We were invited to their home in Virginia many times; Dave and Jack share birthdays, we went with them to Williamsburg, the wedding, and they continue to be a very treasured "connection."

Jack wrote the following about his daughter's wedding:

When Sarah McAllister and David Penny decided to get married, they wanted to get married at Sarah's parents' home near Winchester, Virginia, and they wanted David Simonson to perform the ceremony. Sarah and her parents, Jack and Jane, had traveled to Tanzania several times and had formed a close friendship with the Simonsons.

The day was June 6, 1992, and the setting was the front porch of the McAllister's' federal-style house (circa 1800), overlooking a lush, green hillside. Eunice was seated among the eighteen family members. A harpist, who was seated in the corner of the porch, played background music. It was a hot and humid Virginia day.

Three steps down, on a lower stoop, Dave, robed in his traditional Maasai stole, faced the couple. He talked to this young couple who were both avid outdoor enthusiasts and cautioned them of worshiping nature too much. He advised them instead to always remember God the Creator and to be aware of God's presence in their lives through the Holy Spirit. David likened the Holy Spirit to wind moving through our lives; he said that one cannot see God anymore than one can see a breeze, but one can feel his presence, as one feels a cool breeze. At that moment, we heard music from the harp, but the musician's hands were in her lap. A gentle breeze had moved through the harp strings. This happened several times, and we knew we were blessed with God's presence that day.

Sarah's parents, Sarah, David Penney, David Simonson, me, Jane and Jack McAllister.

Epilogue

"In my Father's house are many mansions...
I go to prepare a place for you"
(John 14:2).

One of the many emails sent after Dave's death came from a young architect, Jerry Murray, who worked with Dave. He expressed this thought: "It would take a pretty big house to contain Dave." My train of thought brought this verse to mind, "The Father's House."

As of August 16, 2010, Dave left our House of Five Circles and was received into the house God had prepared for him. I could visualize Dave admiring the architecture and rejoicing with the Great Architect. This was far easier to imagine than Dave sitting on a cloud playing a harp.

Dave's changing houses has been a blessed move. His years of fading health had kept him limited in so many ways physically. He now moves freely without pain. I miss him deeply, yet rejoice he now has this heavenly home where God may continue to use him.

A beautiful tribute that warmed my heart came from Maria Nhambu, a Tanzanian connection who has been very dear to us. She wrote, "Just like me, I believe that the Tanzanian people that he loved, connected with him deep in their hearts, where love, gratitude, and admiration cannot be put into words. They can only be felt, because they are sacred. Along with my fellow Tanzanians, I mourn his passing, but we know that the land he walked on and toiled in for so many years cannot and will not ever forget his precious gift of unconditional love for us. I am so blessed to have known him and loved him in this way."

This also brings a sort of closure to my memoirs, but not to the memories. Dave and I shared fifty-eight wonderful years together. We both reached our four score years and were blessed with five great children, fifteen grandchildren, and two great-grandchildren.

We are humbled and grateful to our Lord for calling us to share the Good News in Africa. Tanzania has become our home, and its people our family. Who could ask for anything more?

David's grave

Me with some of my grandchildren following Dave's funeral.